Transportation Needs of the Poor

LABOR ECONOMICS AND URBAN STUDIES

Previously published in this series:

WELFARE INCOME AND EMPLOYMENT: An
Economic Analysis of Family Choice
by Elizabeth F. Durbin

THE NEW CAREERS CONCEPT: Potential for
Public Employment of the Poor
by Mark A. Haskell

PRAEGER SPECIAL STUDIES IN
U.S. ECONOMIC AND SOCIAL DEVELOPMENT

Transportation
Needs of the Poor

A CASE STUDY OF NEW YORK CITY

Oscar A. Ornati

with assistance from James W. Whittaker
and Richard Solomon

PRAEGER PUBLISHERS
New York • Washington • London

The purpose of Praeger Special Studies is to make specialized research in U.S. and international economics and politics available to the academic, business, and government communities. For further information, write to the Special Projects Division, Praeger Publishers, Inc., 111 Fourth Avenue, New York, N.Y. 10003.

PRAEGER PUBLISHERS
111 Fourth Avenue, New York, N.Y. 10003, U.S.A.
5, Cromwell Place, London S.W.7, England

Published in the United States of America in 1969
by Praeger Publishers, Inc.

© 1969 by Praeger Publishers, Inc.

Library of Congress Catalog Card Number: 69-19350

Printed in the United States of America

PREFACE

This book is about the transportation needs of
urban poor. It is based primarily on a case study of
New York City, yet its theoretical and policy parts
(Parts I and III) go well beyond the situation of New
York. The book argues that existing public transportation networks in American metropolitan centers of
the third quarter of the twentieth century provide an
unsatisfactory link between the job sites for and the
residences of the poor, forming a barrier to their
employment.

A nation's level of employment, in the aggregate,
is determined by its level of demand for goods and
services, private and public. Fiscal and monetary
adjustments are the tools through which a nation en-
deavors to set a level of aggregate demand in line
with employment and other social goals. Fluctuations
in employment that follow from changes in aggregate
demand occur within a number of parameters that vary
little in the short run. Indeed, the way goods are
produced and the way services are provided are determined by technology and practice.

The "rules" that establish the way in which
social and productive activities are organized are
another influence on the number of jobs that exist at
any time and on the number of jobs that are created
through increases in aggregate demand. Most of the
rules that govern society and the labor market are
probably reasonable and augment the collective well-
being. Some of the rules, however, exist because of
chance or habit. Some do not augment well-being, but
instead account for certain major social problems.
Some social, administrative, and market rules tend to
restrict job opportunities. There are many rules that
determine, at any one time, the level, type, and place
of available jobs. Private and public employers de-
cide on the allocation of workers on the basis of
judgments involving the need and availability of workers of different skill levels and the kind of worker
who can best serve the various requirements of the
institutions and of the work environment. Federal,

state, and municipal laws and ordinances on such
factors as labor standards, occupational safety, and
licensure contribute to the number and selection of
who will be hired. The availability of jobs open to
the poor thus is determined only indirectly and in
the long run by fluctuations in aggregate demand.

In recent years economists and policy-makers concerned with social policy, and in particular with the
problems of poverty, have increasingly turned to the
study of variables that determine more immediately who
does and who does not get hired. A focus on the institutional and locational rigidities of the labor
market in the context of the relatively high growth
rates of the last decade and the persistence of high
levels of unemployment in the cities' slums might give
the impression that I am leading up to an argument
against the aggregate-demand theory of unemployment
and to the presentation of the structuralist approach.
I'm not. Admittedly, the case for creating full employment purely by increasing aggregate demand is a
dubious one. On the other hand, the idea that better
matching of jobs with job-seekers can solve the problem is equally questionable. I'm convinced that the
disagreement between the structural and the aggregate-
demand theorists is merely superficial; that both increased demand and structural change are necessary to
deal with the labor market and the cities' depressed-
area aspect of the poverty problem. It is fair to
say that the "aggregate-demanders" concentrate on the
quantity of work and outputs while the structuralists
concentrate on the quality of workers and the location
of economic enterprise. Usually when the phrases are
contraposed in this manner, they refer to two sides of
the same coin. But the complementarity of the two
approaches to the labor market is not so clear-cut.

By generating additional purchasing power, the
aggregate-demanders provide new jobs--jobs that will
be filled in part by the unemployed. The structual-
ists point out that certain groups of people do not
share equally with other groups the benefits of a
rising demand for labor. In addition to matching individual job-seekers with job openings, the structual-
ist urges the mobilizing of these groups of people,
largely through education and training. This approach
seeks to improve the skills and work habits of these
groups (which do not qualify for any job or only for
jobs for which the demand is low relative to the supply of labor) so that they qualify for jobs for which

the supply of labor is low relative to the demand. The structuralist concerned with the gap between the residences of the poor and job locations has the same objective: He wants to link their residences so that they can offer their labor where the supply is low relative to the demand. The efforts of the structuralist to aid the job-seeker--and especially the job-seeker in the nonwhite, teen-age, and unskilled groups--will provide benefits also for the members of these groups not currently seeking jobs. Three groups of people need attention: the employed, the unemployed members of the labor force, and those not in the labor force. The aggregate-demanders seek to help the first and second of these groups; the structuralists seek to help the second and third.

A similar continuum exists for resources. Stocks of capital, knowledge, and entrepreneurial talent may be categorized as employed, unemployed, and "not in the factor market" (or at least not available in all markets). The absence of resources in certain markets creates the structural interstices that the current thrust of national policy tries to fill.

This spin-off from the structuralist approach, even more than the approach itself, makes structural theory especially suited to economists concerned with poverty. The structural hypothesis does not attempt to deal with poverty per se but rather with the condition of groups containing many individuals who, in addition to being job-seekers, happen to be poor. Here lies its attraction. Whereas the aggregate-demand school is concerned with the "unemployed," the structural school is concerned with the not-employed. The distinction, of course, explains why it would be possible to rise to statistical "full employment" without reducing the extent of poverty. Just as raising aggregate demand could not guarantee a solution to the poverty problem, a general restructuring of the labor market and of employment could not guarantee a solution either, because the bulk of the poor are outside the labor market. The common conception of the underprivileged as workers is no longer just old-fashioned. It's erroneous. It is the fact that many are nonworkers that causes the problem.

What it is that makes nonworkers of many of the poor overlaps with other problems of the poor. The problem of getting to where the jobs are (whether the problem is due to poor transportation or because the

poor live in ghettos) is part of the larger problem
of the lack of mobility of the poor. The social benefits of high labor mobility have been recognized since
Adam Smith, in The Wealth of Nations, inveighed
against "whatever obstructs the free circulation of
labour from one employment to another." Yet, in spite
of a large literature on labor mobility, the physical
problem of getting to work does not seem to have been
considered until the McCone Commission on the Watts
riots ascribed as a cause of the riots the difficulties
that Watts-area residents had in going to work. The
McCone Commission's observation led to other analyses
of the poor's accessibility to work locations and to
private and public experimental transportation arrange-
ments linking distant parts of cities.

This volume is one product of Project Labor Market, which was financed by the City of New York's
Human Resources Administration to study the relation
between poverty and the job market in New York City.
The Project's specific intent was to recommend how a
labor market policy could and should be developed to
help eradicate poverty. Project Labor Market was
carried out at the Graduate School of Business Administration of New York University and is an example of
a larger intellectual and policy concern of many other
schools and institutions. The Project focuses on the
determinants of the supply of and demand for labor in
the short run and on the detailed processes--rather
than results--of the city's market. Travel to work
as a barrier to employment was studied in detail, and
a report entitled An Analysis of the Transportation
Requirements of Residents of Poverty Areas in New York
City was submitted to the Human Resources Administration.

The general findings of that report were summarized in its Foreword, which noted that, without exception, the areas of first-magnitude poverty in New
York City have access to the most comprehensive public
transit plant in the United States. With no more than
a five- or ten-minute walk to or from a transit stop,
it is possible to reach every corner of the city and
most of the inner contiguous suburbs by public transit
from any of the poverty areas; in addition, in no case
does the fare for a one-way trip within the city
boundaries exceed 40 cents. Nevertheless, this incom-
parable transit plant was designed primarily for the
urban middle class of an earlier era and has become
obsolescent for the needs of today's very differently
oriented urban poor.

The research and writing of the first report were done by James W. Whittaker, with the aid of Richard Solomon. They worked closely with other members of the Project's staff. Samuel E. Harris and Miss Elizabeth F. Durbin contributed in writing a summary analysis; Maurice V. Amoye helped with the numerous computations. Other members of the staff also helped.

The Project's report focused primarily on New York City, yet it deals with problems and conditions that exist throughout urban America. The subject of the report is re-presented in this volume in a broader and more detailed context, including an analytical matrix that tries to explain the causes of the anomalies of the New York City transportation network in terms of a general analysis of intraurban spatial distribution. Chapter 1 presents the fundamental dynamics of the model and describes the methodology appropriate to the identification of barriers in traveling to work. Chapter 2 describes the New York City transportation system and the extent to which the poor use it. Chapter 3 describes the ways the poor travel to work. Chapter 4 reports on the results of the analysis and identifies the poor's accessibility to areas of employment in terms of time, cost, and complexity. Specific recommendations for rerouting buses and other improvements in service in the New York City system are presented in Chapter 5. Experiences in other cities are described in Chapter 6.

The fundamental rationale for publishing this study at this time rests on the important need to reduce the large number of travel-to-work inconveniences because of their relevance to the job search and job-holding patterns of the poor. This study ends, therefore, with an analysis in Chapter 7 of broad remedial strategies meant to assure a better future link between the job sites and the residences of the poor.

CONTENTS

LIST OF TABLES

LIST OF FIGURES

FIGURES IN THE APPENDIX

PART I

THE SETTING OF THE PROBLEM

CHAPTER **1** INTRODUCTION

Knowing how the poor can get jobs means knowing how they can get to work. To know this about the poor of the second half of the twentieth century calls for focusing on the city and the anomalies of the city's public transportation network.* Indeed, it is true that, for example, a resident of central Brooklyn traveling to nearby industrial districts only four miles away--via one of the nation's most efficient transit systems--finds the journey longer and more complicated than a trip to the Bronx, fifteen miles away. Anomalies of this type appear throughout American cities. In most cases, they relate to the journey that residents of poverty areas must make to centers of employment where they conceivably might find jobs.

Policies aimed at reducing employment-related poverty must respond to the self-evident fact that travel inconvenience is a barrier to employment. The extent of this barrier is not known. Nor has any estimate been made of the degree to which increasing the convenience of travel can reduce employment-related poverty. Nor is it argued that because a route is complicated, time-consuming, or requires payment of multiple fares, it represents a sole or a major or a permanent barrier to a job-holder. Simply put, the premise of this study is that accessibility to place of employment as perceived by a job-seeker, is a determining factor of job search and job-keeping patterns. This is particularly true for the poor, who are more likely to be unfamiliar with a city's complicated transportation network. Given this

---

*As explained earlier, this volume is a product of a case study of New York City. Throughout the study the reader will find references to New York City's five boroughs, or sections: Manhattan, Brooklyn, Queens, the Bronx, and Staten Island.

premise, the first step is to identify the specific
barriers that exist.

That barriers exist in Los Angeles, the nation's
most expansive and sprawling city, does not come as
much of a surprise. But New York, which has the
world's largest and most efficient (if not most com-
modious) transportation system, might be expected to
have no significant problems. An analysis of patterns of intrametropolitan development suggests the
opposite. Thus this case study of the difficulty of
the poor in traveling to work must start with an
analysis of the impact of urban growth patterns on
metropolitan transport.

If significant barriers or inconveniences in
traveling to employment locations are found, the
second step must be a search for solutions. Suggested remedies involve consideration of financing,
planning, public administration, political organization, and so forth. Clearly, the needed action will
differ from city to city; yet some similarities exist.
The case study of the transportation needs of the
poor in New York City leads us to the formulation of
certain specific recommendations for that city. But
the methodology used to identify accessibility barriers is general and suggests categories of causes and
solutions. These will be discussed in Chapter 7.

INTRAMETROPOLITAN DEVELOPMENTS

The available knowledge of spatial organization
of the urban economy has come from policy problems
associated with the regulation of land resources, the
provision of public facilities, and the work of local
planners. The efforts of the latter have led to "a
realization that the internal organization of the
city and the directions in which it tended to change
were manifestations of powerful social and economic
factors that determined land use patterns, the movement of goods and people and the distribution of in-
frastructure."[1] Yet, this realization has not brought
with it a unified theory with which one can truly
move and on which one can build an integrated explanation of accessibility to employment sites. Indeed,
Edgar M. Hoover, who has most meticulously studied
the urban scene, finds no ideal or equilibrium state.
For him, spatial structure "represents"a snapshot

of current states of mutual adjustments. Impacts of
one change upon another and spatial adjustments take
time because long lived physical facilities, habits,
social and business ties, and political commitments
are entailed."[2]

What is known about the urban structure has been
drawn from the theory of industrial location, market
area analyses, rent theory, and so forth. Linking
together the many bits and pieces from the large and
elegant literature gives at least one stable datum--
the notion of the Central Business District (CBD)--
and a set of recognized relationships that can be
adapted to explain a multitude of urban conditions
linked into the spatial context. Clearly, to study
the relationship of poor people's residences to their
access to employment sites, we must look at the major
determinants of household and firm location. This
can be done in the aggregate for the general experience of American cities. Following a little-known
article by Charles Leven,[3] we present a gross summary
of what is known.

A SYNOPTIC VIEW OF
URBAN SPATIAL DEVELOPMENT

Two established facts set the outer limits of
our "model-analysis-description": (1) American
cities continue to grow larger, and (2) to sustain
a labor force large enough and varied enough to permit industry-mix shifts, cities have to have a population of at least 0.25 million. Indeed, we are
interested only in large cities, because they have
the primary difficulties of access to job locations.

The relationships involved in the analysis are:
(1) the relationship between technology and the cost
of land, which is viewed as making space cheaper as
the individual household and employer move away from
the city's center; (2) individual preference as to
"access," which is viewed as a preference of individuals to keep the time-distance between where they
live and where they work or play as small as possible;
(3) the taxpayer's preference for paying lower, rather
than higher, prices for increasing quantities of all
types of public services, including public transportation; and (4) the preference of people to live near
people who are like, rather than unlike, themselves.

With the above considerations in mind, a synopsis
of urban development with reference to transportation
can be traced through five typical stages. (See
Figure 1.)

In Stage 1 (Figure 1A) the city is condensed;
the Central Business District is compact. Production
and distribution activities are tied together closely;
the factory, the store, the church, the saloon, and
City Hall are all within easy reach of each other.
The rich occupy land with advantageous accessibility
and settle around the CBD. The poor take the cheaper
low-access land and settle around the rich residences.
Most employment opportunities are located in the CBD
and right next door to where the poor live. Most
manufacturing establishments that service the CBD
settle where land is cheaper. The poor walk to work,
some walking through the richer residential areas.
"This is the Chicago of the 70's and 80's--the great
days of LaSalle Street and Prairie Avenue, surrounded
by the stock yards."[4] The city's internal transportation system provides no problem and has little influence in determining locations.

In Stage 2 (Figure 1B) large avenues with
streetcars and, later, buses, and the commuter railroads, play an important role. Middle-income groups
split off into outlying city locations, while the
poor are brought into closer contact with the rich
who live around the Central Business District. To
regain the social distance that they lost, the rich
leapfrog over the middle-class residences to outlying
commuter suburbs that spring up along the railroads'
radial, which has reduced the access to the CBD.
Most employment sites remain in easy access to the
poor. The poor shop close to where they live and not
far from where they work. The rich come in along the
radials to do both. Public entertainment remains in
or near the CBD, and the suburbs are mainly dormi-
tories and sites for religious institutions.

A few employment centers develop outside the
areas inhabited by the middle class not far from the
railway lines; they are easily staffed, provide no
problems, and are the harbingers of later stages.
Stage 2 is well represented in the development from
the turn of the century to the early 1920's--in "the
apartment houses of the Bronx, the six family flats
of Chicago, the two family flats of Cleveland"[5] and
the two-story houses of Cambridge and Somerville
around Boston.

In Stage 3 (Figure 1C) automobile ownership by
the higher-income groups begins to determine the
city's spatial organization. The rich keep moving out
of the city to fill a first suburban ring. Thereby
they maintain their social distance, escape the tax
burden of the central city, and boost the creation of
suburban governments. The inner ring of wealthy residences is narrowed; on one hand, mansions are taken
over by the businesses of the CBD, and, on the other
hand, by the poor. New York City's Fifth Avenue, with
its stores and hotels moving up to 59th Street and the
slums of Harlem moving down to 108th Street, is an almost perfect paradigm of this phenomenon.

In Stage 3 the poor and the middle class take
over almost all of the central city. Work places
rapidly increase in number and in distance from the
original CBD. Some work locations develop in middle-
class areas and occasionally outside the first suburban circle. For most of the poor, access to work
sites is still not a problem because most jobs, as
well as shopping and entertainment areas, are linked
by the transportation network developed in Stage 2.

Job locations in middle-class areas are also
generally accessible to the poor, who now reside mostly along the avenues used by the middle class to move
back and forth to the CBD. A city's road network may
be a grid or a radial, but the important fact is that
buses, streetcars, and subways are plentiful, having
been built in response to middle-class pressures.
Stage 3 represents most of the cities of the 1930's.
The diagram approximates a representation of Indianap-
olis.

Stage 4 (Figure 1D) is characterized by wide-
spread automobile ownership (except by the poor) and
by the leapfrogging of the middle classes, who now
create a new (the second) suburban ring. The second
ring develops because the middle class, like the rich,
wants to maintain its social distance and, again, because access costs have gone down. In Stage 4 there
is still only limited outward movement of job sites;
yet the poor's access to them has worsened. The public transportation network, whether grid or radial,
is less effective because the new employment locations are set up in response to automobile and truck
routes--indeed, the expressways now replace the railroads. Travel into and out of the CBD is easy and
rapid, but travel within the central city is more
difficult. Travel across and within the second

Figure 1

A SYNOPTIC VIEW OF METROPOLITAN GROWTH

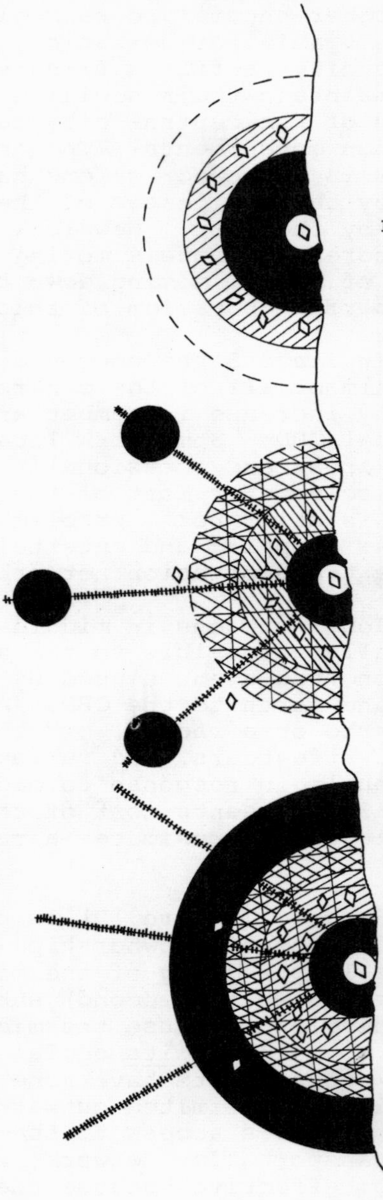

The rich live at high-access locations
around the CBD and the poor cluster
about job locations.

Figure 1A

The middle class split off to outlying central-city locations
serviced by the internal transportation grid. The rich relocate
to commuter suburbs serviced by
the railroads.

Figure 1B

The rich fill the first suburban
ring. The middle class and the
poor take over most of the central
city.

Figure 1C

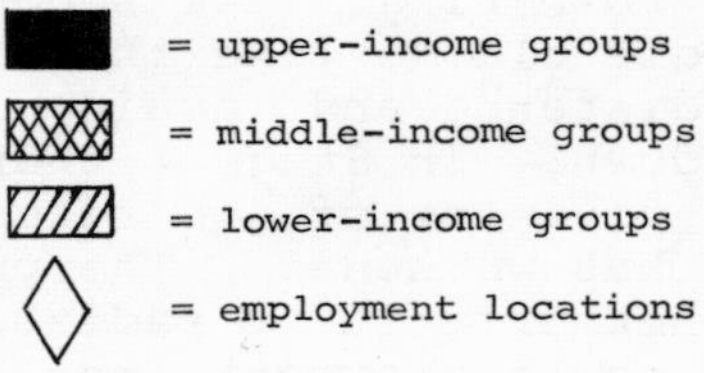

█████ = upper-income groups

▨▨▨▨ = middle-income groups

▨▨▨▨ = lower-income groups

◇ = employment locations

8

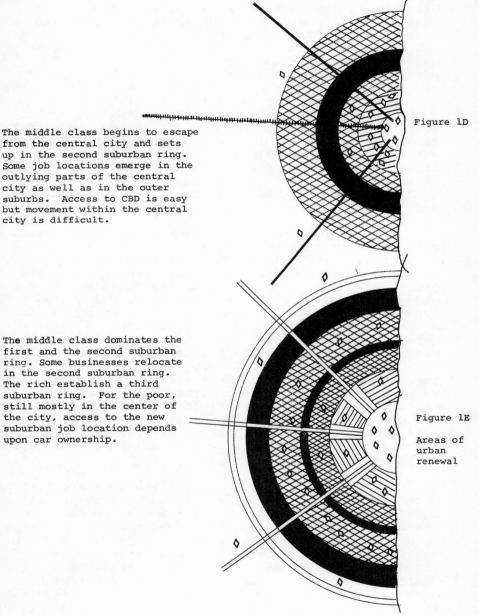

The middle class begins to escape from the central city and sets up in the second suburban ring. Some job locations emerge in the outlying parts of the central city as well as in the outer suburbs. Access to CBD is easy but movement within the central city is difficult.

Figure 1D

The middle class dominates the first and the second suburban ring. Some businesses relocate in the second suburban ring. The rich establish a third suburban ring. For the poor, still mostly in the center of the city, access to the new suburban job location depends upon car ownership.

Figure 1E

Areas of urban renewal

suburban ring is almost impossible without an automobile. Suburban manufacturing employment sites, at
least at first, are small and scattered. Outlying
shopping centers develop and create satellite CBD's,
but these are geared primarily to the middle-class
buyers who come to them by car and for whom large
parking lots are provided. To go from the expanded
central-city poverty ring to work in the middle-class
suburbs without a car is difficult, as there are no
systematic political pressures to extend the public
transportation network for those involved in "reverse
commuting." Stage 4 is the prototype of the large
city in the late 1940's and early 1950's. Modified
forms of Stage 4 represent contemporary urban places
of between 0.5 and 1 million people. In the late
1960's, Rochester, New York; Albuquerque, New Mexico;
and Denver, Colorado, all qualify as Stage 4 cities.

Stage 5 (Figure 1E) represents the large metropolitan centers of the 1960's. It repeats the dynamics of earlier stages: The rich move out of the
first suburban ring--increasingly taken over by the
poor at the near end and the middle class at the far
end--to escape to a new third--and later fourth--
suburban ring. In the second suburban ring the middle classes are not faring well, as their public
services--mostly schools for which they clamor--are
costlier. To broaden the tax base of their towns
and unincorporated areas, they invite industry from
the central city. Businesses are eager to move out,
as transportation in the central city is getting
costlier and municipal services are deteriorating under the strain of increased density of the poor population and of their demands for services. New suburban
industrial districts form in the less-populated parts
of the second suburban ring.

The residential locations of the poor and their
work sites are now no longer linked by transportation.
Indeed, expressways that provide access to the CBD
where the middle classes shop have improved, but they
do not increase the ability of the poor to reach job
sites. Generally, there is already fair access to
the CBD's shopping and entertainment facilities. The
central-city public transportation network remains
unchanged in size and routes, unless it deteriorates
from overuse and obsolescence. When it expands, it
is to care for the needs of the middle class in the
first suburban ring. The poverty areas of the central
city show little change except for the beginning

outmigration of the poor, often accelerated by urban
renewal along the expressways. Some of the poor move
out to the second suburban ring and settle in its
older and denser parts. Having moved to the suburbs,
they have improved their situation somewhat. In most
cases they are still far from the industrial parks
that provide the bulk of the unskilled employment potential. These poor have settled in the least densely
populated areas, and there still is no way to move
across and within the second ring except by automobile.

     In the model sketched above, time and space inter-
twine. We see that: (1) job sites are least location-
bound over time; (2) the residential locations of the
poor--in respect to job location--are more rigidly
fixed; and (3) the public transportation network is
the most fixed of the three. From looking at the
model we can say to the poor: If you take the route
you are likely to take, from the place you are likely
to come from, getting to work is hard. The measure of
fit of the hypotheses, implied in the dynamics of the
model, will vary from city to city with the history,
the physical contour, the character of government, the
administration control over public transportation, and
the industry-mix and employer-size-mix of each. So
will the travel inconvenience of the job-seeker vary.

FACTORS THAT COMPLICATE
TRAVEL TO WORK

     The degree of travel inconvenience of the job-
seeking poor is very much affected by the geographic
distribution of job sites. If potential employment
sites are concentrated, the task of the job-seeker is
eased once he gets to the general area. Holding on to
jobs that are hard to get to is easier when job sites
are contiguous. Then transportation habits develop
faster (car pooling is easier) and, eventually, the
public transportation network adjusts to service-
concentrated employment locations. When, jobs are
scattered, the problem of access to job sites is com-
pounded--particularly so for the job-seeker.

     In New York City, for instance, particularly
outside Manhattan, there is no one area of unskilled
work, nor any one large-scale employer; New York's
manufacturing, the usual source of blue-collar work,
is typically small-scale and, in recent years, increasingly decentralized. This means that it is

practically impossible for any one individual to check
a significant number of possible job openings; by the
same token, the probability of finding a job at any
one firm is fairly small. The added travel inconvenience of searching for employment in cities with
scattered, small job sites thus adds significantly to
the time and cost for the poor and, therefore, serves
as a meaningful barrier to employment.

    Job-seeking and employment also involve dealing
with institutions ancillary to the labor market. Private and public employment agencies tend to cluster in
the older and larger CBD. The field offices of governmental labor-standards regulatory agencies, voca-
tional guidance·centers, etc. are also located in the
CBD. In most cities the poor's accessibility via the
public transportation network is thus handicapped more
by lack of familiarity with the transportation network
than by the absence of connecting routes. Indeed, the
poor are much less handicapped in reaching the shopping
areas of the CBD. The difficulty lies in going from
the employment agency to the site of potential employment.

    Ethnic makeup and degree of residential segrega-
tion of each city will also influence any test of the
hypotheses suggested earlier. The residential segregation of Negroes has become one of the most important
issues involved in today's "equality" revolution.
Doing away with this form of segregation, it is argued, will contribute to the reduction in white-non-
white differential in employment opportunity.[6] As
far as this analysis is concerned, what needs clari-
fication is whether there is indeed greater difficulty
in job accessibility between low-income whites and
low-income nonwhites. Related issues--such as whether
residential segregation itself reduces the total stock
of available jobs, discrimination in employment,
schooling, etc.--are not part of this study.

    The issue of whether differential accessibility
to job location between whites and nonwhites exists
can be recast by asking whether the historico-spatial
development traced earlier can predict the presence
of a racially linked differential job accessibility.
The answer appears to be negative. Contrary to popular belief, residential segregation of Negroes cannot
be explained primarily in terms of average income and
occupational differential between whites and nonwhites.
C. and A. F. Taeuber[7] and A. H. Pascal[8] have shown

that little of the Negro residential segregation vis-
à-vis the white population can be explained this way.

　　To shape our analysis to suit the problem (rather
than pursue it as an intellectual challenge), we must
trace the issue of different racial job accessibility
further through two related questions: (1) Is car
ownership, which we have seen to be important in
shaping urban spatial distribution and in general
travel-to-work patterns, differentiable in terms of
race? (2) Are the job-search patterns of nonwhites
different from those of white poverty-area residents?
The answers are clear: Keeping income constant, on
the average, Negroes own fewer cars (not more, as the
mythology about blacks buying pink Cadillacs would
have it), and nonwhites have more extensive--although
less successful--job-search patterns. Thus we can
conclude, a priori, even though our previous analysis
did not suggest it, that job accessibility presents
more of a problem for nonwhites than for whites and
that travel inconvenience to work sites is compounded
for the Negro job-seeker.

METHODOLOGY FOR DETERMINING
ACCESS TO JOB SITES

　　The general methodology through which one can
establish the poor's relative ease of access to job
sites is simple and easily applicable to any large
center. The crucial dynamics of the model presented
earlier suggests a decreasing flexibility, over a
period of time, in job sites, the residential location
of the poor, and the transportation network. This is
what needs to be tested. Fundamentally, the overlaying
of three maps is required: one pinpointing employment
potential of the poor, one identifying residential
areas of the low-income population, and one tracing
the routes of the public transportation network.

　　There are complications with the construction of
each of these maps and variations among cities in the
availability of needed data. Employment locations can
be derived from land use or zoning maps, supplemented
with information drawn from local business directories.
Such sources generally yield data only on employment
locations; they need adjustment to identify locations
of employment open particularly to the poor. To
achieve the latter, the investigator can be guided by
general notions as well as specific data on the

industry's proportion of skilled to unskilled labor
and on the average wages paid in the industry. The
judgment of the investigator is, of course, crucial.

The residential areas of the low-income population can be plotted from census tract data through
the cumulation of adjacent tracts of low median income.
A "low" median income--to say nothing of income distribution below the median--is as difficult to define
as the meaning of "being poor." In other contexts I
have discussed extensively the problem of the definition of poverty and how such a definition affects the
problem under discussion.[9] Here it is enough to say
that the choice of the income cut-off must reflect
social judgments and the particular city's over-all
income average; ideally, several income cut-offs should
be used to identify the "band of poverty" involved.
In many cities the identification of poverty neighborhoods is already available from various agencies involved in antipoverty activities. In certain cities
data are available to distinguish areas of first- and
second-magnitude poverty. This is the case in New York
City, and the case study presented in this volume re-
lies heavily on the identification by the Human Resources Administration of areas of poverty of first
magnitude. (See Appendix A for the detailed methodology.)

Maps describing the routes and the stops of the
public transportation network are generally available
from the local transit authority. In other cases,
either they do not exist or they cover only those
routes serviced by some such form of fixed plant as
subways or trolleys. In such cases the investigator
must construct a new map, either directly or in combination with existing maps. The overlaid maps will
readily indicate whether accessibility of employment
sites through the public transportation network
exists or not.

Establishing the pure and simple existence of
accessibility is not enough. A judgment as to its
convenience for the poor--relative to the nonpoor--is
also needed. The relative convenience of a public travel system is determined by time, cost and complexity.
These factors can be established by drawing boundaries
along these three dimensions. (See the delineation of
these boundaries for New York City in Appendix Figure
5 in Appendix C.) In addition, cities with large
areas of poverty probably require detailed studies of

the transportation situation in specific poverty
neighborhoods. The largest conglomerate of first-
magnitude poverty areas in the New York study was re-
divided into four subareas, each of which is locally
recognized as having certain traits of neighborhood
commonality. (See map in Appendix A.)

In the following chapters the situation of New
York City and the transportation requirements of residents of poverty areas are discussed in detail.

NOTES

1. H. S. Perloff and L. Wingo, Jr., ed., "Introduction," Issues in Urban Economics (Baltimore: The
Johns Hopkins Press, 1968), p. 17.

2. E. M. Hoover, "The Evolving Form and Organization of the Metropolis," Perloff and Wingo, ibid.,
p. 238.

3. C. Leven, "Trends in Metropolitan Growth and
City Form," Education for Architectural Technology,
an American Institute of Architects Educational Research Project Conference.

4. Ibid., p. 8.

5. Ibid.

6. J. F. Kain, "Testimony," Employment and Manpower Problems in the Cities, Hearings, Joint Economic
Committee, U.S. Congress, May, 1968, p. 65.

7. C. Taeuber and A. F. Taeuber, Negroes in
Cities, Residential Segregation and Neighborhood
Change (Chicago: Aldine Publishing Co., 1965).

8. A. H. Pascal, "The Economics of Housing
Segregation," abstracts of papers presented at the
December, 1965, meetings (New York: Econometric
Society, 1966), p. 2.

9. O. A. Ornati, Poverty Amid Affluence (New
York: Twentieth Century Fund, 1966), p. 26.

PART II

THE CASE OF NEW YORK CITY

CHAPTER **2** THE NEW YORK CITY
PUBLIC TRANSPORTATION
SYSTEM AND ITS USE
BY THE POOR

The New York City Transit Authority operates
236.7 route miles of rapid transit subway and elevated lines, and with its operating subsidiary, the
Manhattan and Bronx Surface Transit Operating Authority, covers virtually all of Manhattan, the Bronx,
Staten Island, Brooklyn, and half of Queens with bus
lines. In addition, extensive bus routes in Queens
are run by several private companies.

The transit map indicates that there are few
places more than a short walk from a transit stop.
But as the map also implies, the system is quite complex and, in spite of a fare structure based mainly
on a single price, it varies in its fare impact;
therein lies the problem of mobility for the poor and
the uneducated.

New York is one of the few cities in the United
States in which public transit is the dominant mode
for journey-to-work trips. The rapid transit network
has been developed with the two Manhattan Central
Business Districts as its primary focuses and downtown Brooklyn as a secondary focus. The subway-
elevated lines, however complex, do give fairly convenient access to these points from all of Manhattan,
most of Brooklyn and the Bronx, and about half of
Queens.

Note: As indicated in the Preface, the detailed
analysis of New York City was ably carried out by
James W. Whittaker, who is responsible for a major
part of the writing in Part II.

TRENDS IN USE OF
PUBLIC TRANSPORTATION

Rapid Transit

From 1955 to 1960, the total number of annual
passengers on the subway system declined 2.4 per cent.
In Manhattan, passengers using stations in poverty
areas declined more than double the system rate (5.1
per cent), while passengers in nonpoverty areas
showed only 1.4 per cent decline over the five-year
period.* (See Table 1.)   In the Bronx, however,
nearly the opposite occurred. While total riding in
the Bronx declined at exactly the same rate as did
the over-all city system, poverty areas showed a
modest decline (0.6 per cent) while other areas declined 3.4 per cent. This may be due to other in-
fluences. During this period, service on the Third
Avenue Elevated was curtailed in Manhattan, causing
very sharp declines at all remaining Third Avenue El
stations in the Bronx. Further, the decline in total
number of passengers on the Bronx Concourse line more
than accounts for the decline in the total number of
passengers in nonpoverty areas of the Bronx. As this
line accounted for the largest number of passengers
in the nonpoverty areas, yet is very close to the
first-magnitude poverty areas for much of its length
(as well as bordering other poverty areas of second
magnitude), it exerted a deceptively disproportionate
effect on subway-riding trends in the nonpoverty
areas. Other factors must also be considered, such
as the relative decline in the West Side of Manhattan
vis-à-vis the East Side and the decline in the Thirty-
fourth Street area as a shopping center.

In central Brooklyn, passenger use of stations
in poverty areas in the western portion showed modest
declines of 2.8 per cent and 2.6 per cent in Analysis
Areas A and B, respectively. Poverty areas in the
eastern portion experienced increases of 5.9 per cent
and 3.0 per cent (Analysis Areas C and D).

_____

*In this analysis, nonpoverty areas are all
areas other than those of first magnitude. Accordingly, fewer poverty areas are included.

Table 1

PER CENT CHANGE IN NUMBER OF
RAPID TRANSIT PASSENGERS IN NEW YORK CITY

Annual	1955-60	1960-65
TOTAL SUBWAY SYSTEM	-2.4%	+1.3%
CENTRAL BROOKLYN	+.6	-5.1
Analysis Area A	-2.8	-7.3
Analysis Area A'	-3.6	-3.8
Analysis Area B	-2.6	-5.3
Analysis Area C	+5.9	-3.6
Analysis Area D	+3.0	-1.7
MANHATTAN	-2.8	-0.7
Poverty Areas	-5.1	-6.2
Nonpoverty Areas	-1.4	+2.6
BRONX	-2.4	+0.2
Poverty Areas	-0.6	-2.4
Nonpoverty Areas	-3.4	+1.7

Daily: October "peg" count	1960-65	
	6AM-9AM	24 Hours
MANHATTAN	-12.2	-0.4
Poverty Areas	-15.2	-5.9
Nonpoverty Areas	-10.1	+2.7
BRONX	-7.0	+0.1
Poverty Areas	-9.6	-1.0
Nonpoverty Areas	-5.8	+0.6
CENTRAL BROOKLYN	-14.8	-5.6
Analysis Area A	-16.6	-7.3
Analysis Area A'	-15.7	-6.2
Analysis Area B	+ 2.2	-2.3
Analysis Area C	-18.4	-5.6
Analysis Area D	-15.1	-3.4

Source: Appendix B.

21

For the period 1960 to 1965, a more detailed
analysis of riding trends was conducted. The annual
data for the total system showed an increase of 1.3
per cent in total passengers. In both Manhattan and
the Bronx annual passenger counts in nonpoverty areas
showed an increase greater than the system average
(2.6 per cent and 1.7 per cent respectively), while
passengers in poverty areas declined 6.2 per cent in
Manhattan and 2.4 per cent in the Bronx. All of the
poverty areas in central Brooklyn showed declines;
these declines were greater in the western sectors.
(See Table 1.)

Analysis of passenger volumes during the peak
morning hours on a typical weekday in 1960 and 1965
was even more significant. Passengers boarding trains
during the three-hour peak period declined 15.2 per
cent in poverty areas in Manhattan compared with a
drop of 10.1 per cent in nonpoverty areas. In the
Bronx, the peak period declines were 9.6 per cent in
poverty areas and only 5.8 per cent in nonpoverty
areas. Central Brooklyn experienced some of the
sharpest declines in passengers in all but one sector.

Accordingly, it must be concluded that subway
stations in poverty areas suffered greater decreases
in travel than nonpoverty areas and more significant
decreases during peak hours. For twenty-four-hour
periods some of the nonpoverty areas lost passengers.

Buses

Data for bus passengers are not obtainable for
specific areas. The only figures available from the
Transit Authority are annual revenue passengers for
each bus line. Accordingly, eight bus routes in
Brooklyn were selected for comparative analysis with
other routes in that division. The selected routes
operate for the most part in the poverty areas of
central Brooklyn. It must be remembered, however,
that these routes also extend beyond the areas of our
specific interest. Table 2 shows the trend of revenue
passengers on the selected poverty bus routes as well
as the total Brooklyn bus division for the years 1955,
1960, and 1965. During the period 1955-60 the poverty
routes suffered a decline of 3 per cent in passenger
volume while the balance of the Brooklyn system declined only 0.04 per cent. From 1960 to 1965 the same
poverty routes declined at the rate of 2 per cent while
the balance of the system experienced a 7.4 per cent
increase in passengers.

Table 2

PER CENT CHANGE IN NUMBER OF
BUS PASSENGERS IN CENTRAL BROOKLYN

Selected Routes in Central Brooklyn[a]	Per Cent Change	
	1955-60	1960-65
14 Pitkin Avenue	(1.5)	6.0
19 Carlton Avenue	(26.9)	(6.3)
38 De Kalb Avenue	(6.8)	(2.3)
48 Lorimer Street	(6.6)	(3.2)
52 Gates Avenue	(3.4)	(5.4)
54 Myrtle Avenue	(18.0)	(4.0)
65 Bergen Street	10.2	(8.0)
69 Vanderbilt Avenue	4.7	(8.1)
Total	(3.0)	(2.0)
All Other Routes	(.04)	7.4

[a]Routes 48 and 65 were operated with trolley coaches until July 26, 1960.

Source: New York City Transit Authority, Transit Record.

USE OF SUBURBAN RAILROADS

The suburban railroad network is not utilized to any substantial degree by residents of poverty areas in New York City. In the following chapter on journey-to-work travel as determined from the 1960 Census, the use of commuter rail service in the study areas was found to be so small that the data are simply included together with bus and subway under "public transportation" as the means of transport.

Use of the suburban railroad is also a minor factor where total travel is considered. Recent surveys show that in southeastern Queens only about 2 per cent of the trips to the Manhattan CBD are by railroad.* Of course, most travel originating in this area is not destined to Manhattan--63 per cent of all trips are entirely within Queens, for which the railroad is least useful. Fifteen per cent of all travel is destined to Nassau County, accounting for nearly twice as many trips as to the Manhattan CBD. Nevertheless, only 3.2 per cent of all trips to Nassau are by rail. For travel to one specific area (the Huntington and Northport area), the railroad did accommodate 24 per cent of all trips, but the total number of trips to this area was not significant. Nearly half of all trips to Nassau County are destined to nearby Valley Stream and Malverne--travel for which there are no recorded rail trips.

It is interesting to take a closer look at this area with respect to rail service. The Atlantic branch of the Long Island Rail Road bisects the South Jamaica area lengthwise and could provide the most direct access to the Manhattan CBD, downtown Brooklyn, and a variety of points in Nassau County. In the mid-1950's there were several stations located within the South Jamaica poverty area. In the late 1950's, however, the railroad in this area was elevated upon an embankment in order to eliminate all grade crossings. At the same time all stations within the South Jamaica poverty area were eliminated. Indeed, the only station that remains on this line today, Locust Manor, is not

---

*Southern Queens includes the South Jamaica poverty area and the adjacent areas of Hillside, St. Albans, Cambria Heights, Springfield Gardens, and Laurelton.

at the original site.   The new station is located adjacent to the recently constructed Rochdale Village
complex, a development consisting of middle-income
cooperative apartments with a high proportion of re-
tired persons.   Accordingly, the only remaining station on the Atlantic branch is located at a point that
makes it convenient to an area least likely to use the
service.   Although the railroad offers the potential
of providing rapid access to several distant areas of
employment opportunity, it offers absolutely no service
in the South Jamaica poverty area.

There are many reasons for changes in the use of
the public transportation network.   Route changes,
changes in automobile ownership and use, and changes
in shopping and employment locations all contribute.
The relative impact of each of these has not been
factored out in any definite sense as no reconstruc-
tion of available data would permit it.

We are certain that the decrease in the use of
public transportation by the poor is not entirely
traceable to one seemingly obvious cause--population
decreases.   Indeed, while we still have no unchal-
lengeable data as to populations living in poverty
areas, all evidence points to decreases less marked
than the decrease in the use of public transportation.
The following analysis of the characteristics of
journey-to-work travel from poverty areas will throw
additional light on the use of the public transportation network by the poor.

CHAPTER **3** JOURNEY-TO-WORK
TRAVEL IN POVERTY
AREAS

Not all poor live in poverty areas. Nor, contrary to the impression conveyed by studies of urban
poverty of the early 1960's, are the poor entirely
frozen in the old city slums. In fact, a "scatteration" of the poor from the old slums to new slums is
going on at all times. Yet what is significant is
that the movement of the poor, relative to the movement of jobs, is a slower one. Analysis of the problem of travel to work from formally designated
poverty areas, besides being the only area for which
data are available, is sufficient for testing the
fundamental dynamics of the situation.

GENERAL CHARACTERISTICS
OF POVERTY AREAS

There are more than 1.6 million people living in
areas designated as first-magnitude poverty in the
City of New York--more than 21 per cent of the total
population of the city.* The majority of the population in these areas is concentrated in the Bedford-
Stuyvesant-Brownsville-East New York complex in central Brooklyn, accounting for 45.5 per cent of the
total. Harlem is the next largest concentration with
26.5 per cent, followed by poverty areas in the Bronx
(Croton Park-East Tremont-South Bronx areas) that account for 24.1 per cent of total poverty-area population. The remaining areas are located in South
Jamaica (2.4 per cent), and the Lower East Side (2
per cent).

----

*See Appendix A for definitions of poverty areas.

Forty-four per cent of the total population of all poverty areas is nonwhite. The proportion varies widely, however, according to the particular section. (See Table 3.) At the extremes, nearly 85 per cent of South Jamaica is nonwhite, while the easternmost part of the Brooklyn complex is a low 7.5 per cent nonwhite. Even in Manhattan the differences are considerable. Harlem is two-thirds nonwhite while the Lower East Side is only 10.6 per cent nonwhite.

LOCATIONS OF JOBS

The 1960 Census shows a total of more than 622,000 employed workers residing in the poverty areas that are the concern of this study. These workers constituted 90 per cent of the total civilian labor force identified in the census. The employment locations and travel patterns of these workers can be--albeit in a limited fashion--characterized as follows:

Principal Areas of Employment

The majority of workers living in both poverty and nonpoverty areas are employed either in Manhattan or the borough in which they reside. Table 4 shows the percentage of workers employed in these areas for each of the neighborhoods under study. Significantly, in Harlem and the Lower East Side, more than 78 per cent of all workers were employed in the Borough of Manhattan. In the Bronx, only about 41 per cent of all workers were employed in Manhattan, while 38 per cent were employed within the borough of the Bronx. In the five poverty analysis areas of Brooklyn, employment of workers in Manhattan ranged from 20 per cent to 29 per cent, while the proportion of workers employed in Brooklyn ranged from 54 per cent to 61 per cent. In the South Jamaica poverty area, more than 21 per cent of workers were employed in Manhattan, while about 52 per cent were employed in Queens.

The data for poverty areas contrast markedly with similar data for the middle-income areas in Flushing and Richmond Hill. For both of these areas, a significantly larger percentage of workers were employed in Manhattan than for poverty areas in Brooklyn and Queens, and roughly proportionately fewer workers were employed in Queens. Thus, we must conclude that middle-income employees in Queens have a much stronger

Table 3

POPULATION OF NEW YORK CITY POVERTY AREAS,
TOTAL AND NONWHITE

	Population	% of Total Population of Borough	Nonwhite Population	Nonwhite % of Total Population of Poverty Area	% Distribution Population of Poverty Areas
Harlem	440,171	25.9	291,829	66.3	26.5
Lower East Side	33,418	2.0	3,549	10.6	2.0
Crotona Pk.-E.Tremont	105,958	7.4	40,915	38.6	6.4
South Bronx	295,112	20.7	68,017	23.0	17.7
Brooklyn Analysis Area A	172,210	6.6	72,220	41.9	10.4
" " B	119,440	4.5	32,546	27.2	7.2
" " C	262,246	10.0	158,913	60.6	15.8
" " D	161,394	6.1	34,222	21.2	9.7
" " E	39,766	1.5	3,000	7.5	2.4
South Jamaica	30,915	1.7	26,184	84.6	1.9
Total Poverty Areas	1,660,666	21.3	731,395	44.0	100.0

Source: U.S. Census of 1960.

Table 4

LOCATION OF EMPLOYMENT
IN NEW YORK CITY

	Per cent of Workers Employed in:	
	Manhattan	Borough of Residence
Poverty Areas		
Harlem	78.4	78.4
Lower East Side	79.9	79.9
Crotona Pk.-E. Tremont	40.7	37.9
South Bronx	41.7	37.8
Brooklyn Analysis Area A	23.6	58.6
" " B	20.4	61.1
" " C	22.6	57.4
" " D	28.8	54.0
" " E	28.1	55.3
South Jamaica	21.4	51.7
Middle-income Areas		
Flushing	38.6	43.8
Richmond Hill	36.8	39.3
City and Borough Averages		
New York City	48.6	-
Bronx	44.8	37.8
Brooklyn	32.0	53.4
Manhattan	82.0	82.0
Queens	41.4	37.0
Staten Island	30.3	52.8

Source: See Apendix B, Table 1.

29

orientation to Manhattan employment locations than do
those living in the poverty areas of Brooklyn and
Queens.

For Harlem, the Lower East Side, and the poverty
areas of the Bronx, however, the Borough of Manhattan
predominates as the employment area. If these latter
poverty areas are compared with their respective borough averages, however, Manhattan employment is still
clearly shown to be less attractive. Although 78 per
cent of workers in Harlem are employed in Manhattan,
the average for all workers residing in Manhattan is
82 per cent. In the Bronx, the percentage of workers
employed in Manhattan was 40.7 per cent and 41.7 per
cent for the Crotona Park-East Tremont and the South
Bronx areas, respectively. These compare with the
slightly but statistically significant higher average
for the Bronx of 44.8 per cent. The proportion of
workers employed in the Bronx, however, is exactly the
same (37.8 per cent) for both poverty areas and the
borough as a whole.

We must conclude that even where the poverty
areas are located within Manhattan or very close to
it (as in the case of the Bronx) the relative attraction of Manhattan employment locations is less for
low-income workers than for residents of nonpoverty
neighborhoods.

Other Employment Locations

Table 5 shows the percentage distribution of
workers by borough or county in the New York Standard
Metropolitan Statistical Area (SMSA). Very few workers
from poverty areas are employed outside their boroughs
of residence or the Borough of Manhattan. The only
notable exceptions are in poverty areas in Brooklyn
and Queens. In South Jamaica, nearly 8 per cent are
employed in Nassau County, while 6.2 per cent travel
in the opposite direction, to Brooklyn. In the
Brooklyn poverty areas (Bedford-Stuyvesant-Browns-
ville-East New York complex) very few workers travel
to Nassau County—only 1.4 per cent in Analysis Areas
C and D—while travel to employment locations in
Queens ranges from 3 per cent to 6 per cent.

In middle-income areas in Queens, there is very
little travel in the direction of Nassau County—sur-
prisingly, only 3.8 per cent from Flushing, which is

Table 5

LOCATION OF EMPLOYMENT OF WORKERS RESIDING
IN SELECTED AREAS OF NEW YORK CITY

Per Cent of All Workers Employed In:[a]

	Bronx	Brooklyn	Manhattan	Queens	Staten Island	Nassau	Suffolk	Westchester	Rockland	Outside SMSA	N.R.[b]
Harlem	3.0	2.9	78.4	2.9	.1	.3	.1	.7	.1	2.1	9.4
Lower East Side	1.7	5.5	79.9	2.6	.1	0.5	.1	–	–	2.2	7.4
Crotona Pk.-E. Tremont	37.9	2.7	40.7	3.5	–	.4	–	.1	.1	2.4	12.2
South Bronx	37.8	3.1	41.7	3.8	.1	.4	.1	–	.1	2.2	10.7
Brooklyn Analysis Area A	.8	58.6	23.6	4.0	.1	.9	.2	–	–	1.6	10.2
" " " B	.7	61.1	20.4	6.0	–	.6	.1	–	–	1.5	9.6
" " " C	.7	57.4	22.6	5.5	.1	1.4	.2	–	–	1.4	10.7
" " " D	.8	54.0	28.8	5.4	.1	1.4	.3	–	–	1.4	7.8
" " " E	.6	55.3	28.1	3.0	.1	.8	.3	–	–	1.0	10.8
South Jamaica	1.1	6.2	21.4	51.7	.1	7.9	.6	.1	–	.9	10.0
Middle-Income Areas:											
Flushing	2.6	4.4	38.6	43.8	–	3.8	.3	.6	–	1.4	4.5
Richmond Hill	.7	13.3	36.8	39.3	–	3.1	.5	.2	–	1.3	4.8
City & Borough Averages											
New York City	7.6	20.1	48.6	11.1	1.4	1.6	.2	.8	–	2.0	6.6
Bronx	37.8	2.2	44.8	2.7	–	.5	.1	2.9	.1	2.1	6.8
Brooklyn	.6	53.4	32.0	4.0	.1	1.1	.2	.2	–	1.6	6.8
Manhattan	1.5	2.3	82.0	1.9	.1	.4	.1	.6	.1	2.5	8.5
Queens	1.4	8.6	41.4	37.0	–	4.2	.4	.4	–	1.4	5.2
Staten Island	.2	3.9	30.3	.7	52.8	.1	–	.1	–	6.4	5.5

aIncluding armed forces and places of work not reported.
bPlace of work not reported.

Source: See Appendix B, Table 1.

quite close to the Nassau County boundary. Some orientation toward Brooklyn is apparent, with 13.3 per
cent of workers in Richmond Hill and 4.4 per cent of
workers in Flushing employed in that borough.

Comparison of these areas with the average for
residents of the entire Borough of Queens reveals a
similar pattern. The strongest orientation is toward
Manhattan, while slightly fewer are employed in Queens.
A lesser attraction toward Brooklyn--8.6 per cent--is
followed by only 4.2 per cent employed in Nassau
County.

RELATIONSHIP BETWEEN JOB SITE
AND USE OF PUBLIC TRANSPORTATION

Figure 2 indicates the relationship between
workers employed in their borough of residence and the
average use of public transportation area by area in
poverty and nonpoverty areas. The diagram suggests a
strong and positive relationship between the use of
public transportation and the percentage of employment
in the same borough. The two increase almost proportionately. It must be noted, however, that the plot
points in Figure 2 are clustered according to the location of poverty areas. The highest points on both
scales are Harlem and the Lower East Side, reflecting
the low incidence of automobile ownership in Manhattan
(particularly in the poverty areas) and the combined
attraction of employment within borough of residence
and the unique employment opportunities in the Borough
of Manhattan.

The five poverty analysis areas in Brooklyn occupy the central portion of the scatter diagram, showing
more dependence upon job opportunities outside the
borough of residence (i.e., in Manhattan.) South
Jamaica, with slightly less dependence on public
transportation and somewhat greater dispersion of employment localities, is apparent in the scatter trend
while the middle-income areas of Flushing and Richmond
Hill are at the lower end of both scales. The exception to this pattern is the position occupied by the
two poverty areas in the Bronx, reflecting high dependence upon public transportation but close proximity (and good public transport access) to employment
locations outside that borough, in Manhattan.

Figure 2

RELATIONSHIP BETWEEN PER CENT
OF WORKERS EMPLOYED IN BOROUGH OF
RESIDENCE AND USE OF PUBLIC TRANSPORTATION

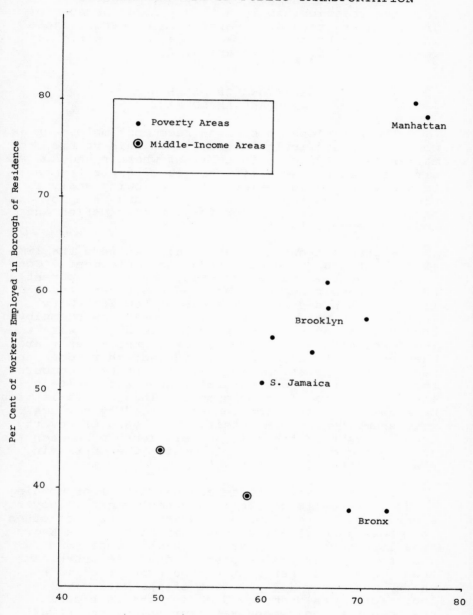

Figure 3 relates the per cent of workers employed in Manhattan to the use of public transportation. Here the relationship is not very clear because of the greater attraction of poverty-area workers to jobs within their borough of residence, as compared with workers in middle-income areas.

RELATIONSHIP BETWEEN
RACE AND EMPLOYMENT

The relationship between race and employment is complex and difficult to trace. In this volume, the matter is raised only in terms of whether and how much differential accessibility to job sites is traceable to social characteristics. The following analysis proceeds at two levels: Employment and unemployment are discussed first, labor force participation and underemployment later.

Figure 4 shows in scatter-diagram form the limited relationship between race and employment. Contrary to what might be expected, there is apparently no relationship between race and employment for those living within the poverty areas of New York City. That is, the per cent of males reported as unemployed does not increase in any perceptible degree with the incidence of nonwhite population of the poverty areas. When nonpoverty areas are considered, there does appear to be a relationship, but it must be remembered that nonpoverty areas naturally have a relatively minor incidence of unemployment. Thus, while it might be a common observation to associate "Negro slums" with unemployment, an intensive analysis of poverty areas shows that there is no relationship between race and the incidence of unemployment. The overriding characteristic is poverty.

The realization that race has little or nothing to do with levels of reported unemployment in poverty areas is not a new finding. Nevertheless, too often the gross generalization has been made that a Negro area is undoubtedly an area of high unemployment. Just the contrary is demonstrated in the South Jamaica area: Nearly 85 per cent of the population is nonwhite, but only 4.3 per cent of the male civilian labor force was unemployed during the last census-- the lowest unemployment rate for any of the poverty areas and less than the average unemployment rate for the city as a whole.

Figure 3

RELATIONSHIP BETWEEN PER CENT OF
NEW YORK CITY WORKERS EMPLOYED IN MANHATTAN
AND USE OF PUBLIC TRANSPORTATION

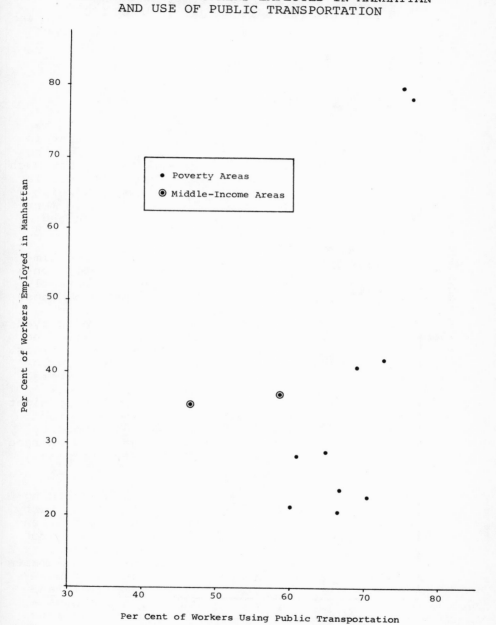

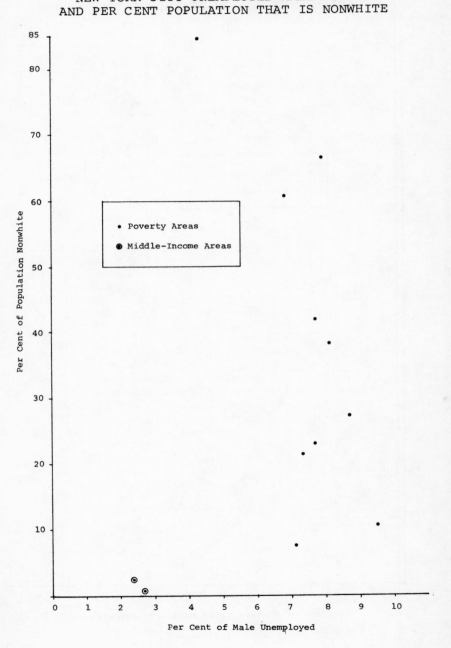

Figure 4

RELATIONSHIP BETWEEN PER CENT OF
NEW YORK CITY UNEMPLOYED MALE WORKERS
AND PER CENT POPULATION THAT IS NONWHITE

Per Cent of Population Nonwhite

- Poverty Areas
- Middle-Income Areas

Per Cent of Male Unemployed

The finding that reported unemployment in poverty
areas does not correlate with race may result from
certain inadequacies in the census data. Clearly, not
all Negro males in the poverty areas are enumerated.
By 1968 all but the most naive have learned that the
rate of unemployment is a very limited datum. Table
6, breaking down unemployment for three poverty areas
(albeit not fully comparable with poverty areas identified so far) in the City, adds some data on some
characteristics of unemployment there and darkens the
picture a good deal. This table shows a rate of unemployment at least twice as high as in the city, a tendency for a greater proportion of the unemployed to
be long-term unemployed, very high rates of teen-age
unemployment, and the fact that one and one-half of
the males of working age are out of the labor force
for each one in a similar situation in the rest of the
city.

The three poverty areas identified are predomi-
nantly Negro, and it is the higher levels of unemployment of these areas that account for part of the higher aggregate level of Negro unemployment throughout
the city. The table also shows that in each of these
three areas the unemployment rate of Puerto Ricans is
even higher.

A more precise measure of unemployment was de-
vised by the U.S. Department of Labor and applied to
the City's poverty neighborhoods for November, 1966.
This measure, in addition to the adjustments described
below, tries to correct for the serious Negro male
census undercount discovered since 1960 and mentioned
above. To measure "subemployment," to those unemployed
in the sense that they are actively looking for work
and unable to find it are added those working only
part-time when they are trying to get full-time work
heads of households (under sixty-five) earning less
than $60 per week while working full-time, and indi-
viduals (under sixty-five) who are not heads of
households and earn less than $56 per week in a full-
time job; also an estimate (about half) of the male
twenty-to-sixty-four group, who, when the census-taker
comes to their door, indicate that they are not in a
job, not in school, not in the Armed Forces, and not
even looking for work.

The subemployment rates for the poverty areas of
the City are also presented in Table 6. As with the
unemployment statistic, the subemployment rate of

Table 6

SELECTED MEASURES OF UNEMPLOYMENT
IN THREE NEW YORK CITY POVERTY AREAS

(November, 1966)

	Central Harlem	East Harlem	Bedford-Stuyvesant	3 Areas Combined
Unemployment[a]	8.1	9.0	6.2	7.5
Puerto Rican Unemployment	11.8	9.7	7.8	9.8
Long-term Unemployed[b]	9.1	13.2	12.5	n.a.
Unemployed Aged 16-21	27.8	25.1	20.0	n.a.
Males Aged 20-64 Not in Labor Force	10.3	10.9	7.7	n.a.
Subemployment	28.6	33.1	27.6	29.1
Puerto Rican Subemployment	28.1	36.9	29.7	33.3

[a]Regular U.S. Department of Labor definition.

[b]Sixteen weeks or more.

Source: U.S. Department of Labor, Special Census of Poverty Areas, November, 1966; U.S. Department of Labor, Labor Force Experience of the Puerto-Rican Worker, Regional Reports No. 9, June, 1968.

Puerto Ricans is higher for all three neighborhoods,
33.3 per cent compared with 29.1 per cent. The rate
is significantly higher in East Harlem (37 per cent),
which is the area of major Puerto Rican concentration.
From the point of view of the problems of the journey
to work, data on subemployment stress the travail of
the job-seeker who lives in these areas.

EFFECT OF INCOME LEVEL
ON TRANSPORTATION MODE

Public Transportation

     Figure 5 shows the relationship between the use
of public transportation for the journey to work and
the proportion of families with incomes under $4,000
for each of the ten poverty areas and two middle-
income areas, and averages for each of the boroughs
and the City of New York. The scatter diagram shows
a very definite trend toward greater use of public
transportation as income declines. At the extremes,
Flushing shows 11.6 per cent of families with incomes
under $4,000 and only 49.9 per cent of all workers
using public transportation for the journey to work.
In Harlem, however, 51.6 per cent of the families had
incomes under $4,000, while more than 76 per cent of
all workers used public transportation to reach their
jobs. For all of the other areas analyzed, it is
evident that the use of public transportation for the
journey to work tends to increase as does the incidence of poverty families.

Automobile Transportation

     Figure 6 shows the relationship between the
availability of automobiles and the incidence of poverty. As might be expected, the per cent of households with at least one automobile available increases
as the per cent of families with incomes under $4,000
decreases. A very strong degree of negative correlation is evident in Figure 6. Of the areas analyzed,
Flushing, which has only 11.6 per cent of families
with incomes under $4,000, shows the highest (75 per
cent) automobile availability for any of the individual neighborhoods. On the other hand, Harlem, with
nearly 52 per cent of families with incomes under
$4,000, and the Lower East Side, with about 50 per
cent under $4,000, both have the lowest availability
of automobiles. Fewer than 15 per cent of households
in these areas have at least one automobile available.

Figure 5

RELATIONSHIP BETWEEN NEW YORK CITY
FAMILY INCOME AND USE OF PUBLIC
TRANSPORTATION FOR THE JOURNEY TO WORK

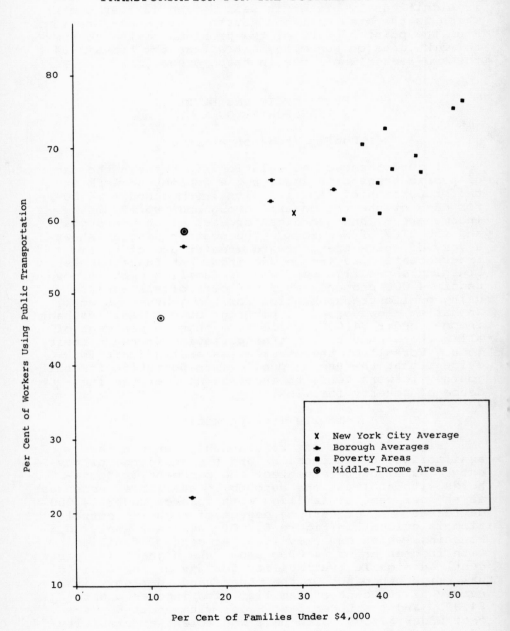

Per Cent of Workers Using Public Transportation

Per Cent of Families Under $4,000

X   New York City Average
◆   Borough Averages
■   Poverty Areas
◉   Middle-Income Areas

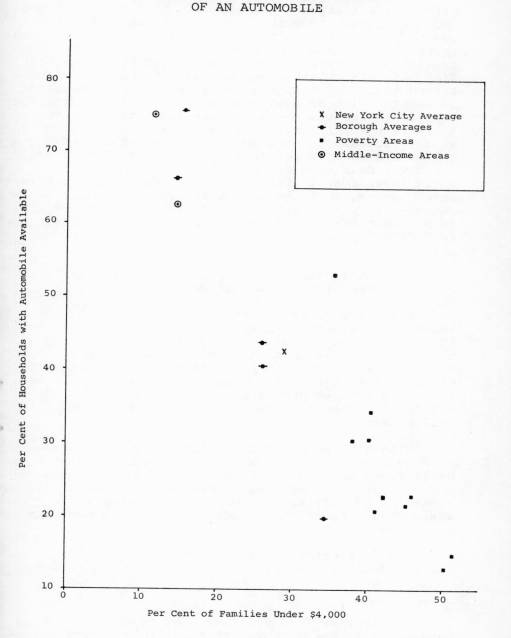

Figure 6

RELATIONSHIP BETWEEN NEW YORK CITY
FAMILY INCOME AND AVAILABILITY
OF AN AUTOMOBILE

X   New York City Average
•   Borough Averages
■   Poverty Areas
◉   Middle-Income Areas

Per Cent of Households with Automobile Available

Per Cent of Families Under $4,000

Figure 7 shows the relationship between automobile availability and the use of public transportation for the journey to work. As might be expected, the use of public transportation is highest in those areas where the percentage of households with an automobile available is lowest, namely Harlem and the Lower East Side. In all other areas, the use of public transportation tends to decline somewhat as the percentage of households with an available automobile increases. The decline in the use of public transportation for the journey to work, however, is not nearly so pronounced as the increase in automobile availability. Thus, while more than 75 per cent of workers in Harlem and the Lower East Side use public transportation and while fewer than 15 per cent of the families in these areas have automobiles, a comparison with South Jamaica shows 53 per cent of families with automobiles and 60 per cent of workers using public transportation to reach their jobs.

RELATIONSHIP BETWEEN NEIGHBORHOOD
STABILITY AND USE OF MASS TRANSIT

A measure of neighborhood stability may be obtained from a determination of the percentage of the 1960 population, five years old and over, residing in the same house as in 1955. These data, shown in Table 7, have been related to percentage changes in the total number of annual rapid transit passengers between the years 1955-60 and 1960-65.* Figure 8 shows the association for seven poverty areas in Brooklyn, Harlem, and the Bronx.

With the exception of Harlem there may be some relationship indicating a tendency toward greater declines in rapid transit usage (for all purposes) as the transiency of an area increases. Similarly, the instances of increased subway riding appear to be associated with neighborhoods having less in-and-out migration.

The scatter chart also shows progressively sharper declines in rapid transit passengers between

---

*Determined from statistics of annual revenue passengers entering subway stations in selected neighborhoods.

Figure 7

RELATIONSHIP BETWEEN NEW YORK CITY
RESIDENTS' USE OF PUBLIC TRANSPORTATION
AND AVAILABILITY OF AN AUTOMOBILE

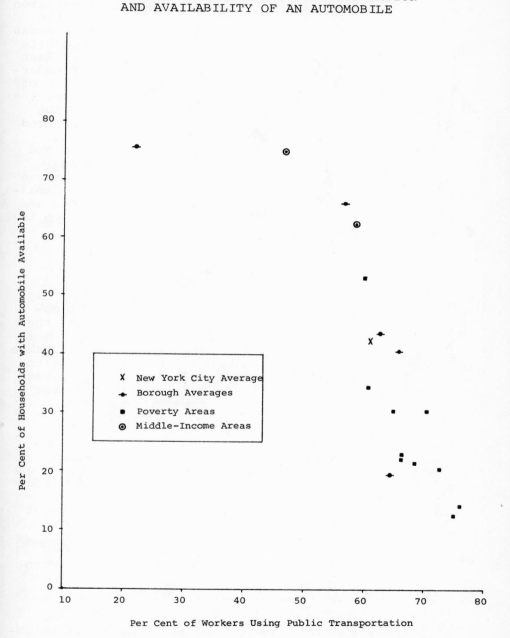

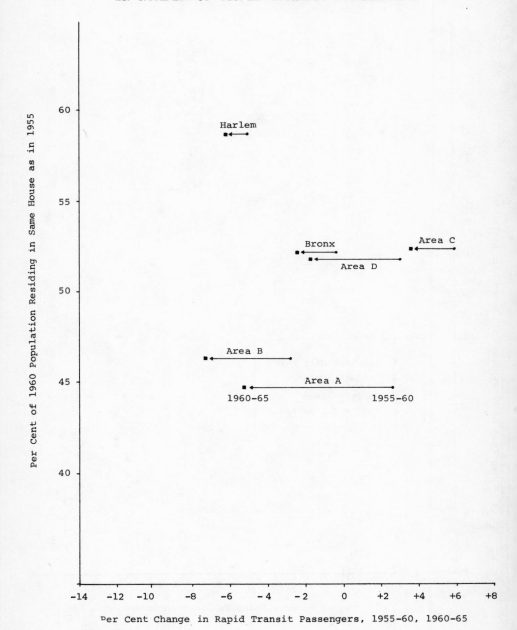

Figure 8

RELATIONSHIP BETWEEN NEIGHBORHOOD
STABILITY IN NEW YORK CITY AND CHANGES
IN NUMBER OF RAPID TRANSIT PASSENGERS

Per Cent Change in Rapid Transit Passengers, 1955-60, 1960-65

Per Cent of 1960 Population Residing in Same House as in 1955

44

Table 7

RELATIONSHIP BETWEEN HOUSEHOLD
MOBILITY AND USE OF
RAPID TRANSIT IN NEW YORK CITY

	% of Households Same House as in 1955	% Increase or (Decrease) in Number of Rapid Transit Passengers Total Annual		Peak Period
		1955-60	1960-65	1960-65
Poverty Areas:				
Harlem	58.7	(5.1)	(6.2)	(15.2)
Lower East Side	52.9			
Crotona Pk.-E. Tremont	52.5 ⎫ 52.2	(.6)	(2.4)	(9.6)
South Bronx	51.9 ⎭			
Brooklyn Analysis Area A	46.3	(2.8)	(7.3)	(16.6)
" " B	44.7	2.6	(5.3)	2.2
" " C	52.4	5.9	(3.6)	(18.4)
" " D	51.8	3.0	(1.7)	(15.1)
Middle-income Areas:				
Flushing	57.0			
Richmond Hill	59.4			
New York City	58.1	(2.4)	1.3	

45

1960 and 1965 as the stability of the areas decreases.
The limited data, however, do not permit the formulation of a definite conclusion.. More analytical work
is required here. However, the following possibilities occur:

(1) A "transit habit" is adopted by a
stabilized population over a period of years.

(2) Different employment characteristics
of a new population require them to seek jobs
in areas difficult to reach by public transit.

CHAPTER **4** FACTORS DETERMINING
ACCESSIBILITY OF
EMPLOYMENT AREAS

OBJECTIVES OF A TRAVEL SYSTEM

The primary objective of any public transportation system is to make possible the movement of people
between place of residence and place of work, shopping,
and recreation in an efficient, rapid, and tightly
scheduled manner. As Manhattan is simultaneously the
dominant work, shopping, and recreational center of
the metropolitan area, this means that Manhattan must
be the hub of the transportation network. Within each
of the surrounding boroughs, however, there are secondary centers, or Central Business Districts, which
must be serviced by the transit system. Thus, the New
York transit system must form efficient linkages between places of work and the dominant (Manhattan) and
secondary CBD's. This is satisfactory for populations
whose needs in respect to place of work correspond
well to the central focus on Manhattan as well as the
secondary focuses on the CBD of other boroughs of the
transportation network. There are, as we have seen,
however, some differences in the intensity of the
Manhattan work orientation held by the poor and nonpoor residing both within and outside Manhattan. For
example, while 39 per cent of the residents of Richmond Hills (a middle-income area of Queens) work in
Manhattan, only 21 per cent of the residents of South
Jamaica (a poverty area in Queens) work in Manhattan.
Similarly, while 95 per cent of Manhattan's workers
who live in nonpoverty areas work in Manhattan, less
than 80 per cent of the workers of Harlem and Lower
East Side poverty areas are employed within the
borough.

These differences in the intensity of the Manhattan work orientation among the poor and nonpoor in
large measure reflect the decreasing significance of
Manhattan as an employment center for relatively low
skilled and unskilled labor. The most important

factor accounting for this decrease has been the decentralization of manufacturing into other boroughs
of the City and surrounding counties of the New York
SMSA.

Because of the different intensity in work orientation to Manhattan of the poor and nonpoor and because of the public transit network orientation toward
middle-class residences, the hypothesis presented in
the introduction can be said to be verified. _In four
of the five boroughs of the city, access to job locations is less convenient_ (more "complex," time-consuming, dearer) _for the poor than the nonpoor_.

It would be unreasonable to assume, however, that
just because a route is complex or time-consuming or
requires a double fare it might provide a distinctive
barrier for a _job-holder_. But, to the _job-seeker,_
especially to one unfamiliar with the system, accessibility (especially the job-seeker's own perception of
accessibility) could be a determining factor in establishing where one is willing to look for work. What
follows, as well as the proposed research described
in the ,section on recommendations for the City of New
York, amplifies the broad conclusions reported above.

IMPORTANCE OF MASS TRANSIT

With minor exceptions, most of the industrial
areas and all of the commercial areas within the four
boroughs analyzed are adjacent to subway stations;
large portions of the Newtown Creek-Long Island City
and the Hunts Point industrial areas are inaccessible
by rapid transit but have fairly complete bus coverage
We were unable to obtain exact employment figures for
these areas or information on employment possibilities
in suburban communities and therefore cannot examine
in detail any correlation between the use of transit
by low-income workers and specific employment areas
other than the generalized discussion in the previous
section.

As the model predicted, it was found that almost
all of the industrial areas within New York City are
inside or contiguous to poverty areas. It is reasonable to assume that a large percentage of low-income
workers employed in these areas who reside nearby walk
to work, but this does not imply that any large proportion of low-income workers in general walk to work.

(See Appendix B.)   Still, in four of the ten poverty areas studied in detail the average percentage of workers who walk to work was higher than the city average; in three out of four boroughs for which comparisons could be made the percentage of workers who walk to work in poverty areas was found higher than the total borough percentages.

Furthermore, while most of the industrial areas are convenient to specific poverty neighborhoods, they are <u>not</u> necessarily convenient to other low-income neighborhoods. This is also true of commercial and retail districts, other than Manhattan's CBD, which has the subfunction of serving its immediate neighborhood. In a city where the automobile has not taken hold as a primary journey-to-work mode, transit has reinforced the pattern of concentrated city development. This reinforcement may be advantageous, however, only for the white-collar middle class who have remained in the City and tend to be employed in concentrated commercial districts. The poor, seeking jobs in low-density industrial areas, require an anomalous transportation system--the low-cost advantages of transit combined with the flexibility of the automobile as used by the higher paid blue-collar industrial worker.

The present transit system sometimes appears to serve only the needs of the poor by accident. The detailed analysis of the central Brooklyn first-magnitude area will show this in detail. (See Figure 3 in Appendix C.) Note that, for example, residents of central Brooklyn Analysis Area A' (northeast corner of downtown section) served by the IND "GG" crosstown subway and BMT Myrtle Avenue El have excellent single-ride access to Coney Island, Queens Boulevard, and Fresh Pond, Queens, and good cross-platform-transfer access to most of the West Side of Manhattan and West Bronx (up to fifteen miles distant). The bus routes in the area, however, which would be expected to complement the rapid transit routes, filling in where the subways and elevated railways do not run, merely supplement the rapid transit routes. Bus routes in the area generally follow these two rapid transit lines only to the Brooklyn boundaries and penetrate parts of the southern and eastern segments of the central Brooklyn poverty area, but not much farther.

Residents of the B area who want to go job-hunt-
ing in the sundry warehouse and manufacturing plants
located along the Brooklyn waterfront's Bush Terminal
area, about two and one-half miles away, require a
complex subway routing, a combination of bus trips, or
both. Getting lost is easy. To get to the Flatlands
district of Brooklyn (three and one-half miles away),
currently being promoted by the city as a future industrial growth area, requires two buses or a complicated (although faster) subway-bus combination.

TRAVEL TO EMPLOYMENT AGENCIES

Most of the private employment agencies are located within three blocks north and south of Forty-
second Street between Third and Eighth Avenues in Manhattan. They are in the heart of the CBD and are, as
revealed by the subway station plot maps, in one of
the most accessible parts of the city by rapid transit. The detailed analysis of transit routings from
central Brooklyn confirms this point for that poverty
area. Almost any Manhattan-bound rapid transit train
on any line in the city will take one to the Forty-
second Street area, either directly or with no more
than one cross-platform transfer.

The New York State specialized employment offices
are clustered in midtown Manhattan in the West Fifties
and in the Fourteenth Street area. Again, both of
these areas present no major problems of access, although they are slightly less convenient to all poverty areas than the Forty-second Street section.
Secondary employment agency areas, both public and
private, are found near Fulton Street in Lower Manhattan and in downtown Brooklyn. All major trunk
lines pass through these sections.

A similar picture is presented upon investigating
the accessibility of potential job sites with the applicant starting out from the employment agency office
As most industrial areas of New York are accessible by
rapid transit, or rapid transit plus one bus, and the
transit system is primarily oriented toward Manhattan,
it follows that few transportation problems would hin-
der a job-applicant's journey by public transit from
the employment agency office to the potential job site
Depending upon the job site, however, his problem of
returning home is no different than that of any applicant traveling to an unfamiliar job site from his home

A more complicated logistics problem could arise if the applicant were to go on to another job interview in a different area. For example, the Hunts Point industrial district is <u>less</u> convenient by transit from the Long Island City area, only four street-miles away, than it is to the Atlantic Avenue section of Brooklyn, some ten <u>transit</u>-miles away. This is in spite of a bus route that traverses all three legs of the nearby Triborough Bridge; the bus goes no farther than the bridge plaza in each borough, providing neither free nor convenient transfers to major rapid transit or bus routes. The purpose of this route is to serve the Hospital, Sanitation Department, and Triborough Bridge and Tunnel Authority facilities on Randall's and Ward's islands. Little thought seems to have been given to extending the bus route across 125th Street, in order to connect with all the north-south subway routes and simultaneously serve Harlem, or along Astoria Boulevard to La Guardia Airport, where there is large employment potential.

USE LIMITATIONS IMPOSED
BY THE FARE STRUCTURE

A map of fare "fronts," irrespective of convenience or travel time, shows that all areas of New York City can be reached from the first-magnitude poverty areas for no more than 40 cents. (See Appendix Figure 5.) This is simply due to the flat fare of 20 cents with free transfer privileges on all the NYCTA rapid transit lines, excluding the Rockaway routes, which charge a double fare of 40 cents.

With a few insignificant exceptions, there are no transfers from subway routes to bus lines.* This places most of the areas of the city not served by rapid transit within a "two-fare" or 40-cent zone from the rapid transit districts (including all the poverty areas).

The general existence of a one-fare "zone" principle for most poverty areas does have a few anomalies

---

*The exceptions are even more insignificant when one counts the total lack of information available on these "free" transfer points. (See section on the information problem in Chapter 5.)

worth considering. The Lower East Side, while within
Manhattan and served by several bus lines penetrating
the Manhattan Central Business Districts (both midtown
and downtown), has a large area that is more than
walking distance from a subway station. The data on
the percentage of workers walking to work in this area
show that more than twice as large a group walk to
work than in all of Manhattan. To travel conveniently
from the Lower East Side to the West Side of Manhattan
or to any other borough requires two fares.* Using
our definitions of complexity and convenience, a large,
densely populated section of the City, only a few
miles from the center, has poorer transit service to
the CBD--to say nothing of the link to work sites outside the CBD--than do such areas as Coney Island, Van
Cortlandt Park in the Bronx, or Jamaica, which are
farther out.

A second anomaly arises when the transit service
in central Brooklyn is analyzed in terms of fare
structure. It was pointed out earlier that certain
sections of East New York are more readily accessible
to the Bronx (under our complexity definition) than
the relatively nearby Long Island City area in Queens.
This could be resolved by taking several buses, as no
bus emanating out of the Brownsville-East New York
area would get much beyond the bus garages at Fresh
Pond or East New York. To make such a trip more convenient (in terms of less time consumed and less complexity) would require paying two fares--one subway,
one bus.

As noted previously, in order to reach relatively
nearby areas in Queens from the Bedford-Stuyvesant-
Bushwick area, at least two and more often three buses
are required. The only crosstown subway, the "GG,"
connecting Brooklyn and Queens, does not serve the
Bedford-Stuyvesant area, touching only on the north-
western corner. (See Appendix Figure 2.) Accordingly,
a time-consuming and costly bus trip is required in
order to reach Forest Hills, Kew Gardens, or Richmond
Hill, which are within a five-mile radius of the center

---

*The only local private transit operation in Man-
hattan, the Avenue B and East Broadway Bus Company, is
found in the Lower East Side. It serves as a feeder
to the Union Square subway and shopping complex.

of Bedford-Stuyvesant. It should be noted at this
point that the analysis of accessibility-to-work sites
is restricted to commercial and public employment.
The availability of employment in household work is
excluded. Both Forest Hills and Kew Gardens are areas
of significant employment for women living in central
Brooklyn.

Through bus routes between Brooklyn and Queens
exist. For example, the No. 53-Metropolitan Avenue
line extends from the Williamsburg Bridge to Jamaica
Avenue and 170th Street in Queens. However, this does
not serve the main poverty areas of central Brooklyn,
touching only the northern part of the Williamsburg
section. Another example of a through route is the
No. 22-Atlantic Avenue line, which does enter the
central Brooklyn area and provides a direct service
route between the East New York section and Jamaica,
but it links primarily residential areas. An extension of this route also serves the Bushwick section,
but a through ride from there to 89th Avenue and
Parsons Boulevard in Queens--an area of greater employment potential--is circuitous and time-consuming.
Accordingly more direct routes are chosen, requiring
multiple fares.

ANALYSIS OF THE ABILITY OF
BROOKLYN POVERTY AREA RESIDENTS
TO REACH JOB AREAS

A detailed analysis of the "accessibility" of six
sections in the central Brooklyn first-magnitude poverty area was made. (See Appendix C.) A complex
route was defined as one requiring other than a cross-
platform transfer on a rapid transit line--i.e., an
involved walk through several passageways and up or
down stairways (usually poorly marked). This presumed
mobility barrier is further discussed in the section
on the information problem, Chapter 5.

The subway plot maps of accessibility for central
Brooklyn indicate that all of Manhattan's West Side
commercial district, the Lower Manhattan Financial
district, and (depending upon the analysis section
chosen) most of Manhattan's East Side are accessible
either on one train or with one cross-platform transfer. Certain parts of the East Side of Manhattan require a "complex" subway transfer from all but the

Brownsville section of central Brooklyn (Analysis
Area D on our maps).

     Using these same standards of complexity, we
found that only Analysis Area D, which is served by
several BMT elevated routes and the IND Fulton Street
line ("A" Train), has good rapid transit access to
nearby areas in Brooklyn and Queens as well as much
of Manhattan. This area, however, has very poor access to most of the Bronx (except the area served by
the IND Concourse "D" line) requiring several complex
and cross-platform changes.

     Residents of the other analysis districts of
central Brooklyn have to perform a fairly complicated
maneuver in order to get to geographically nearby
areas of Brooklyn by rapid transit. Some nearby industrial areas of Queens are best reached by taking a
train that first enters Manhattan and then recrosses
the East River in Midtown, then back to Queens.

     For these poverty areas, it was found that the
bus system, which might be expected to supplement the
inadequate rapid transit system, does not offer any
better routes.

     The bus network in New York has undergone few,
if any, major reroutings since the days when it replaced streetcars. Since rapid transit construction
in New York followed a basic radial pattern along the
lines of the heaviest downtown-oriented streetcar
lines,* it is not surprising to find that the primary
bus lines serving the central Brooklyn area** act as

_____

     *In some cases, the Brooklyn Elevateds were re-
placements, or supplements, to surface electric and
steam railways, which ranged halfway between interurban electric railways and suburban railroads.

     **Almost all of the Brooklyn surface (bus or
trolley) system was operated by the same company,
which ran the BMT rapid transit lines, giving rise to
a bus system feeding the subway and Elevateds rather
than running in competition. The latter was the case
in Manhattan and the Bronx, where the trolleys were run
by a group of companies separate from the rapid transit operator. This may partially explain why Harlem
is better served by buses running to contiguous areas
than is central Brooklyn.

extensions and crosstown <u>feeders</u>, rather than filling
the void for non-CBD oriented transit. The bus routes
follow the patterns of the streetcars they replaced;
the streetcar routes had followed passenger travel
patterns that were developed before the turn of the
century, when today's slum areas were middle- or
upper-income neighborhoods and most of the post-World
War I neighborhoods were open countryside.

Although central Brooklyn is saturated with a
grid of local bus routes, the orientation often lacks
logic from the point of view of passengers' needs. A
comprehensive analysis of all sixty-eight bus routes
in Brooklyn is clearly beyond the scope of this study.
A few examples of inadequacies will have to suffice.

Appendix C shows eight bus routes that traverse,
for most or all of their length, the central Brooklyn
first-magnitude poverty areas. It is immediately apparent that the routes have north-south and east-west
orientation. While this is understandable in view of
the grid street pattern, it is significant that these
transit lines provide neither cohesive access within
the central Brooklyn ghetto nor convenient access to
employment or recreation areas outside the ghetto.

Even more significant is the truncation of these
routes at or near the boundaries of the poverty area.
One is strongly tempted to associate the limits of the
bus routes with the definition of the central Brooklyn
area. Of course, there are other bus lines and a network of subway lines that provide access to other
areas. But our hypothesis remains undisputed: The
system is not geared to the needs of the residents of
central Brooklyn. It appears that the entire orientation remains either purely local (in the case of the
eight lines shown in Appendix C), or CBD-oriented.

It is difficult to escape the conclusion that
racial segregation and isolation are exacerbated by
the mere orientation of the bus routes in central
Brooklyn. While there may have been economic logic
to the design of these routes in an earlier era, the
streetcar routes of Brooklyn no longer serve the needs
of the residents of today's poverty areas. The fact
that streetcars were replaced by buses did not signify
any improvement in service to meet the changing requirements of the newcomers to Bedford-Stuyvesant,
Brownsville, and East New York.

One example of isolation through transit route
design is apparent. The No. 55-Richmond Hill line is
a heavily used route (5 million passengers annually)
serving Richmond Hill, Glendale, and Ridgewood. It
connects with the 54-Myrtle Avenue line, which serves
the Bushwick, Bedford, and downtown areas of Brooklyn.
Although Route 54 is a logical extension of Route 55
(or vice versa), the downtown line carries only 20 per
cent as much passenger volume as Route 55. Significantly, there are no transfer privileges between the
two routes. A trip from Bedford or Bushwick to Richmond Hill requires a double fare. If the destination
is Richmond Hill or nearby Forest Hills, Kew Gardens,
or Hillside, requiring another connecting bus, the
one-way fare is 60 cents. (The Myrtle Avenue Elevated
which traverses the northern part of central Brooklyn,
also terminates just across the Queens boundary at a
cemetery, not far from the break between the No. 54
and No. 55 bus routes.)

Another example of the nonadaptation of bus
routes to emerging travel needs is the case of Route
R7, which traverses the Verrazano-Narrows Bridge from
Brooklyn to Staten Island. There are three possible
bus connections with this route on the Brooklyn side
(Fort Hamilton area), but there are no transfer privileges. Routes 37 and 63 provide access between the
bridge line and downtown Brooklyn but no coordination
has been effected. Thus if a resident of Bedford-
Stuyvesant, Bushwick, or East New York decides to
travel to Staten Island by bus, he is obliged to pay
at least two fares and more likely three. This means
that a resident of a poverty area would pay $1.20
daily to reach a job in the only borough of the City
that promises substantial industrial expansion. (Considering the present minimum wage, such a cost consti-
tutes a sizable portion of the earning power of
poverty-level workers.)

The third possible connection is with the Number
64 route, which connects Fort Hamilton with Coney
Island. There are two barriers here; this route ends
six blocks short of the Staten Island route, which
means both a double fare and a triple bus ride in order to travel from Coney Island to Staten Island.
Although not otherwise considered in this study, Coney
Island contains a first-magnitude poverty area that is
thereby "isolated" from job opportunities in the growing industrial areas of Staten Island, in spite of the
existence of several bus and rapid transit routes
serving Coney Island.

The terminal for the R7 bus in Fort Hamilton was
chosen to provide a connection with the Fourth Avenue
subway line, which is a relatively slow local line.*
If the R7 bus were extended to connect with the 59th
Street station (about one and one-half miles), a
faster route to Manhattan would be possible. More
important, however, would be the improved accessibility to other parts of Brooklyn. The Sea Beach Express
would provide convenient access to neighborhoods as
far away as Coney Island. Poverty areas in parts of
central Brooklyn and Coney Island would be linked with
locations in Staten Island for a total one-way fare of
40 cents within reasonable travel time.

The terminal of the R7 bus in Staten Island is
another area requiring further study. While the route
penetrates fairly far into Staten Island, it does not
reach the areas of industrial potential along the
Arthur Kill, nor are there any reasonable connections
with the very substantial industrial complexes along
the New Jersey side of this channel. A limited-stop
bus line originating at the 59th Street Station in
Brooklyn, traversing the Verrazano Bridge and the
breadth of the Island, could obtain sufficient travel
speed to reach important industrial locations in
Elizabeth, New Jersey, within tolerable travel time.
A recent experimental morning and evening express bus
(Route R8X) from Port Richmond, Staten Island, to
Borough Hall, Brooklyn, demonstrates the technique of
a limited-stop bus operation. Unfortunately, this
route operates in the reverse direction of the needs
of any Brooklyn residents who might wish to travel to
Staten Island. Further, the very limited service,
lengthy schedule, and poor location of the Brooklyn
terminus mitigate any possible advantages of this
service for travel between Staten Island and central
Brooklyn.

Significant in the context of the relationship
between accessibility to work and decision-making in
transit affairs is the fact that since the field work
for this study was completed, a new bus line linking

---

*The present terminal was chosen, apparently, on
the basis of minimizing the number of bus-miles necessary to provide the service (thus minimizing the cost
of operations). The increased operating cost of extending the route must be considered against the social benefits of improved service.

Staten Island to Manhattan has been instituted.   But
this new line again by-passes all of the residential
locations of the poor, linking only three minor
CBD's.

CONCLUSION

     The above examples of travel inconveniences in
the nation's most comprehensive transit system are in
part due to the sheer complexity of the system.   If
the travel inconvenience factor appeared with equal
frequency in the journey-to-work trip for the nonpoor,
then the system's complexity could perhaps be used to
account for all travel inconveniences.   There are,
however, too many examples in which the system has
made modifications to increase the convenience factor
in the travel of the nonpoor to accept such an over-
simplified explanation.   In addition, the absence of
universal free transfers between bus and subways in
an otherwise heavily subsidized transit system (as
well as the almost total absence of public knowledge
about the few available free transfers) strongly re-
inforces the general conclusion that the system is
largely unresponsive to the needs of the poor.

     The seriousness of the City's neglect of the
transportation needs of the poor has been dramatized
by the recent defiant attempts of Dr. Thomas W.
Matthew to respond to these needs in a limited fashion
in both South Jamaica and Harlem.   In the summer of
1967 Dr. Matthew, a Negro neurosurgeon running a South
Jamaica hospital, began operating a private bus line
without a franchise.   The line links the area that our
field survey clearly indicated as lacking convenient
public transportation.   Dr. Matthew estimated that his
"bus line" represents a transportation link that could
benefit about 50,000 Negroes.   Though the intent of
mentioning this development was not to support necessarily the approach of Dr. Matthew, our field analysis
does in fact verify the need to which his efforts have
been directed.   In fact, it might even be said that
our recommendations suggest that the City follow the
lead of Dr. Matthew on a more comprehensive and systematic basis.   These recommendations are discussed
in the next chapter.

CHAPTER **5** RECOMMENDATIONS
FOR NEW YORK CITY

MODIFICATIONS OF PUBLIC
TRANSPORT SERVICES

The New York field study reveals the need for
certain public transport services that are presently
unavailable to residents of New York City's major
poverty areas. In addition, certain existing services
could be modified in order to serve better the needs
of ghetto residents.

It is recommended that at least six new express
bus routes be established on an experimental basis to
serve residents of central Brooklyn and central Harlem, and possibly an additional route that would serve
the South Bronx poverty areas. (The proposed routes
are shown in Figure 4 in Appendix C.)

Three of these routes would serve a limited number of pick-up areas in the Bedford-Stuyvesant-
Brownsville sections of Brooklyn, while three other
routes would originate in the 125th Street central
Harlem area. The recommended new routes are:

(1) Central Brooklyn-Staten Island via Gowanus
     Expressway, Verrazano Bridge, Staten Island
     Expressway, to (a) Port Richmond and Bayonne,
     (b) Elizabeth (via Goethal's Bridge).

(2) Central Brooklyn-Kennedy International and
     Hempstead via Conduit Boulevard, Sunrise
     Highway, and Peninsula Boulevard.

(3) Central Harlem-Central Brooklyn via 125th
     St., Triborough Bridge, Astoria, Long Island
     City, Greenpoint, and Williamsburg.

(4) Central Harlem-Hunts Point (Bronx Terminal
     Market) via 125th St., Triborough Bridge,
     Bruckner Expressway, and Hunts Point Avenue.

59

(5) <u>South Jamaica-Central Harlem</u> via Jamaica,
Van Wyck Expressway Extension, Northern
Boulevard, La Guardia, Grand Central Parkway
(access road), Triboro Bridge, 125th Street.

(6) <u>Central Harlem-Bergen County</u> via 125th
Street, Amsterdam Avenue, George Washington
Bridge, State Highway No. 4, to Bergen Mall
and Garden State Plaza shopping centers and
Fair Lawn Industrial Park.

A possible seventh route would serve the South
Bronx area, with express operation via the Throgs
Neck Bridge, Clearview Expressway, and Jericho Turn-
pike to Hempstead.

The Staten Island route would provide access to
the only borough of the City that has substantial industrial growth potential. One leg of this route
would serve existing nonresidential concentrations in
the Port Richmond area. After careful study, it
might be desirable to extend it across the Bayonne
Bridge to the U.S. Naval Supply Depot. The other
branch would follow the Staten Island Expressway directly to the Goethal's Bridge and serve the large
industrial complex in the vicinity of Elizabeth and
Linden, New Jersey.

The Kennedy International Airport route would
serve the large maintenance, fueling, and cargo areas
at that site, which generate substantial employment.
In addition, it would provide access to the planned
industrial park to be established in the City-owned
vacant areas on the fringes of Kennedy Airport. Although much shorter than the Staten Island route,
this line should also be a limited-stop operation.
It could be combined with an express bus service between central Brooklyn and the town of Hempstead in
Nassau County. This service should connect with, or
be incorporated into, the present poverty bus routes
in that area. This would provide access to industrial
areas in Nassau County for residents of central
Brooklyn.

The Central Harlem-Central Brooklyn route would
provide a much-needed link between two poverty areas
that have common needs for access to the commercial
and industrial areas along the route in Long Island
City and the Greenpoint section. This would also
provide a convenient transfer to the Welfare Island

bus, which serves the institutional complex located
there. The route should operate with a limited number of stops on 125th Street in Harlem, run nonstop
via the Triborough Bridge, provide a major transfer
connection in Astoria, then run nonstop to the Long
Island City area, where stops should be selected after
careful study of the employment locations in that vicinity. The route should continue in this fashion
through the Greenpoint section and terminate in the
Bedford-Stuyvesant-Brownsville area.

A Central Harlem-South Jamaica service would provide a limited-stop, no-transfer service between these
important poverty areas. While useful as a direct
connection, it would serve to reduce drastically the
travel time between such areas as central Harlem and
Astoria, La Guardia Airport (an important employment
center), and Jamaica. Residents of the South Jamaica
area would also enjoy direct service to these employment areas.

Direct service between Harlem and the modern
shopping centers and industrial parks in Bergen County
would greatly reduce travel time by public transport
and enable residents of Harlem to obtain employment in
these areas where low-skilled jobs are available. At
present, a trip between eastern Harlem and the Fair
Lawn Industrial Park requires a slow crosstown bus
ride, which runs local to the George Washington Bridge
Bus Terminal where more time is lost in changing to
infrequent suburban buses. This service is very limited for residents of Harlem who are at the disadvantage of having to travel in the opposite direction of
peak service during normal working hours.

In the Bedford-Stuyvesant-Bushwick sections of
central Brooklyn, it is much too difficult to reach
nearby sections of Queens, while there are no non-CBD-
oriented subway routes in the heart of this region.
It is recommended, therefore, that the No. 54-Myrtle
Avenue line be consolidated with the No. 55-Richmond
Hill line. This would provide direct access to Richmond, Glendale, and Ridgewood, as well as better
transfer possibilities for destinations in Kew Gardens, Forest Hills, and Hillside (See Appendix C).

The present R7 bus between the Fort Hamilton
section of Brooklyn and Staten Island should terminate
at the 59th Street subway station instead of at the
end of the Fourth Avenue line. This would provide a
transfer between the bus and the Sea Beach Express

trains, improving access between Staten Island and
the poverty area in Coney Island, as well as to Manhattan. Extension of this route would provide an
opportunity to conduct a definitive benefit-cost
study of the value of the improved service versus the
probable increase in operating expenses. This route
should be coordinated with any new bus service in the
area, such as the recommended limited-stop service
between central Brooklyn, Port Richmond, and Elizabeth.

REVISION OF PUBLIC TRANSPORT
FARE STRUCTURES

The present fare structure of the New York City
Transit System is an accident of history and contains
many anomalies. A complete analysis of the system
interchanges, transfer privileges, and possible connections is much needed. The most that can be recommended here is some equitable adjustment for certain
poverty area services.

In conjunction with the consolidation of Routes
54 and 55 (noted above), free transfers should be instituted between the present Route 55 and all intersecting bus and subway lines. This would provide a
one-fare, two-vehicle ride for residents of the
greater part of Bedford-Stuyvesant and Bushwick reaching Richmond Hill, Forest Hills, Kew Gardens, Hillside, Jamaica, and other nearby locations in Queens.
The importance of this experiment cannot be underes-
timated. There exists today a distinct barrier, both
in terms of available service and multiple fares, to
the accessibility by residents of these ghetto neighborhoods to the neighborhoods of opportunity in
Queens.

Another specific example of fare structure inequality in use of public transit by poverty area
residents for the journey to work exists on the Lower
East Side of Manhattan. This historic low-income
area supports the last privately owned bus service in
Manhattan, which serves as a feeder to the Union
Square subway station complex. Since the subways do
not directly serve the Lower East Side, at least two
fares are necessary to reach employment areas outside
this neighborhood. A system of public subsidy for a
transfer arrangement could do much to alleviate the
transportation burden for workers or potential job-
holders in this important section of the City.

A thorough analysis of the fare structure of the entire New York City transit system would make a most interesting demonstration project under the auspices and financial assistance of the U.S. Department of Housing and Urban Development. The project should be sufficiently funded to conduct a thorough study of bus service, fare structures, and revenue potentials throughout the City.

IMPROVEMENTS IN INFORMATION
AND PROMOTION OF
EXISTING AND MODIFIED SERVICES

A public transit system large enough to serve New York City must necessarily be complex. The need for a large number of routes, extending as much as fifteen miles from one end of the city to another, means a complicated system at the outset. Add to this a similarity of certain station names on different routes serving a common intersecting street, the need for certain labyrinthine stations at intersecting routes, and the problems of engineering feasibility and basic economics in laying out passageways in areas where preexisting utilities and other obstructions interfere, and the result is a network of corridors, platforms, routes, and trains that defies understanding by the novice passenger.

If the subways are baffling in their proliferation of physical facilities, the bus routes are even more difficult to understand because of the lack of physical structure. Indeed, one would not even know that a particular street has bus service until he comes across a clearly indicated stop or observes a bus making a stop.

While it may be reasoned that seven million daily riders manage to find their way, this tells us nothing about the possible information barriers that preclude those who are not presently using the system. The following criticism is based entirely on observation of the system, not a detailed survey.

First, there is no complete map of transit service in New York City. There is a rapid transit map showing subway and elevated routes and stations against a very simplified city outline map, but even major streets are omitted, making it most difficult to locate the best route to a particular destination

that is unfamiliar to the passenger who may have only
a street address for the location. There are also
"bus service guides" for many of the surface routes,
but each one is limited to an individual route. It
is, therefore, impossible to determine the proper
route or combination of routes necessary for a particular trip unless the passenger is in possession of
the right combination of such service guides (or the
total assortment of guides). The latter possibility
is most improbable as maps and service guides are not
available for passenger distribution on the vehicles.
Worse, the bus guides are not even posted for observation in the vehicles.

Further, the signs marking both vehicles and
passageways are wholly inadequate. While some recent
improvements at bus stops in certain selected areas
resulted in very readable maps of the route(s) serving
these stops, the vehicles themselves carry only final
destination signs--no indication of the main thorough-
fares or routes taken to reach it.

Certain complex stations where two or more subway
routes intersect--such as Union Square and Times
Square--present major problems. Nevertheless, it is
possible to improve the present arrangement through
the judicious use of carefully designed signs and
diagrams. Much progress has been made on approaching
this problem in certain foreign transit operations.
The Paris metro, for example, is well-known for the
use of electrically lighted maps of the system, which,
at the touch of a button, show the passenger where he
is and indicate the correct route and stations at
which it is necessary to change trains to reach his
station of destination. The Milan subway system
provides maps in the stations that indicate which exit
to use for access to major streets.

It is recommended that a complete transit map be
designed for the City of New York including all bus
(public and private) and rapid transit routes, major
terminals, and major street background. This is not
an impossible task, but printing in large quantities
for public distribution will cost a substantial sum.
Accordingly, it might be desirable to issue it in
separate sheets for each borough sector and Manhattan.
(It is significant that design and distribution of a
good public transit map--as will be seen in the next
chapter--was a significant aspect of the Watts demonstration project.)

The map should be available for public distribution at all public terminal facilities for a modest charge and distributed free at agencies that are concerned with employment in poverty areas.

NEED FOR IMPROVED
QUALITY OF SERVICE

This study did not attempt a detailed analysis of transit travel time and frequency of service throughout the system. This is a formidable task and unnecessary for our immediate objective--the identification of barriers to the mobility of labor in New York City. It is possible, however, to make several generalizations based upon system observation and limited study of rapid transit and bus schedules.

The present philosophy of transit-service scheduling appears to be based on the maximization of passenger utilization of vehicles. In other words, if one ten-car A train every fifteen minutes after midnight can possibly accommodate all passengers who appear on the station platforms, that is the extent of the service offered. But in the largest metropolitan area in the world, it is not unreasonable to anticipate substantial travel volumes at all hours of the night. And a standing load at 1 A.M. is absurd, by any standard! A major benefit-cost study of increased service during off-peak hours is very much needed.

SUMMARY OF RECOMMENDED
FURTHER RESEARCH

Several references have been made in this study to the need for further study. Any worthwhile investigation that proceeds to break new ground inevitably opens up areas of research needs that were not obvious at the outset and therefore not incorporated into the original research. The following summary of such needs is now obvious.

(1) A major poverty-area bus demonstration project is required to test the feasibility of providing public transport service for the journey to work for residents of poverty areas in New York City who presently face barriers to employment due to relative immobility.

(2)   A major study of the public transit fare
structure is very much in order. The present structure is an accident of history--certain area advantages exist due entirely to precedent, not logic.
Other areas suffer double or triple fares due to lack
of attention to the needs of the population.

(3)   The quality of service--its frequency and
speed--needs a thorough examination. There are undoubtedly ways of speeding the journey to work in
many sections of the City within the fiscal capabil-
ity of the City.

PART III

THE NATURE OF THE SOLUTIONS

CHAPTER **6** PROBLEMS AND
EXPERIMENTS IN
VARIOUS CITIES

The immediate causes and the approximate dimensions of the difficulties the poor have in traveling
to work throughout the nation were recently summarized
by Sumner Myers of the Institute of Public Administration as stemming from the fact that almost everybody who can afford a car has one. Only 57 per cent
of families earning less than $4,000 own a car; more
than two thirds of these cars are seven years old or
older and are about to be removed from the highways
as unsafe. The downtown orientation of public transportation networks and the length and complexity of
off-central bus travel contribute to the difficulties
of these low-income families. Basing his analysis on
Washington, D.C. data, Myers suggests as a "rule of
thumb" that the bus user's potential labor market is
one third smaller than that of the auto owner, other
things being equal. Obviously other things are not
equal, and any national dimension is at most approximate.

Enough data are available to argue that the model
suggested earlier is more than a generalized descrip-
tion. The problems of New York City are not unique.
The new availability of federal funds for research and
experimentation in urban and suburban transportation
indicates that the problem is a general one. It is
now clear that the public transit system of most
cities provides a very limited link between job sites
and the residences of the poor. For the poor this is
a real handicap to employment. There is no attempt to
quantify this handicap. Given available data and the
state of research, it is not even possible to rank the
transportation problem among the other problems of the
poor. Obviously, much more than transportation is
needed to improve the labor market income of the poor.
Indeed, scattered data suggest that even where transportation for the poor has been improved--as in
Watts--the net increase in employment is not large.

Yet, improvement in transportation to work for the
poor is a worthy objective, which must be tackled
area by area.

In this chapter, the problems and experiences of
three areas are reported briefly. The first section
focuses on the broad aspects of transportation needs
in the whole New York Metropolitan Region and expands
on the situation of the city proper. The second section reports on the Watts experiment in Los Angeles.
The third reports the result of experiments linking
employment and residences in suburban areas.

THE NEW YORK METROPOLITAN REGION

The linking of homesites with work sites is less
of a problem when the whole metropolitan region is
analyzed than when parts of the city are looked at
separately. In the twenty-two counties lying in
those portions of New York, New Jersey, and Connecti-
cut that make up the Tri-State Transportation Area of
the region, there is no serious problem of access to
employment for most of the population.

Manufacturing employers with large scale require-
ments--particularly those whose production or ware-
housing requirements call for one-level arrangements--
and those needing large contingents of unskilled labor
have been moving to the suburbs. Employer relocation
is dictated by a multiplicity of forces--cost of land,
level of taxation and service, etc.--operating
throughout the nation.

Many major employers have in the years after
World War II picked a plant site with almost no reference to the residential location of the labor force.
Often employers, in deciding on a location, are concerned with the preference of their top administrative
and scientific personnel and therefore search for communities with good homes and highly rated schools.
Rarely is there a similar concern for production,
maintenance, or clerical workers.

The availability of the automobile to most of the
population has in fact proven the wisdom of the employers' decision. On the other hand, such site decisions have tightened the constraints on a minority of
the low-income population; even on a regional basis,
three quarters of the households earning less than
$4,000 a year have no private vehicles available.

As in other large metropolitan regions, the regional picture is characterized by the following.

(1)   There is a surplus outside the City of low-skilled, low-wage jobs, as against low-income workers, amounting to as much as 100,000 units.

(2)   Low-income people living outside the City have an even more marked propensity to work in the county of their residence than those in the city.

(3)   "Reverse commuting" (i.e., travel to work outside the City), which involves more than 10 per cent of all heads of households, drops to less than 4 per cent for the low-income population, in spite of the large suburban employment potentials for this group.

(4)   There is a slow but continuing "scatteration" of low-income households away from the older cities of the region.

Knowledge of the travel characteristics of the low-income population of the region was developed by the Tri-State Transportation Commission through a 1 per cent home interview survey carried out in 1963, which was compared with census data.[1] The study confirmed and detailed the general disadvantage of the area's low-income population. In addition, it emphasized that:

(1)   While the manufacturing industry stands out as a major employer of all income categories, low-income heads of households are equally distributed across all industry groups.

(2)   Residential mobility is more related to age than to income, with low-income groups being as mobile as high-income groups.

(3)   Employment changes for the employed population do not seem related to income; when movement in and out of employment is added to employment mobility--as expected--the low-income population is much more mobile.

(4)   Car ownership is the key factor in travel

behavior outside the City. The study notes:

> The need for an automobile in areas
> of generally poor transit service is
> demonstrated by the fact that as much
> as 53 per cent of the employed and 33
> per cent of the unemployed low income
> households residing outside New York
> City have at least one private auto
> available.[2]

(5) Frequency of travel is--as expected--lower
     for low-income groups even when the data are
     analyzed on a per person rather than a per
     family basis.

(6) The distance traveled to work by employed
     low-income heads of households is signifi-
     cantly lower irrespective of auto ownership,
     and lower for the low-income population of
     the areas surrounding the City than for
     those in the City.

(7) Travel time, in absolute terms, of employed
     heads of low-income households is lower than
     that of the middle- or higher-income groups
     and lower for the noncity than for the City
     poor.

(8) Mass transit outside the City is, even more
     than in the City, geared entirely to the
     various CBD's or suburban shopping centers.
     The extent to which the mass transportation
     system is inefficient in serving job loca-
     tions is attested to by the fact that even
     long-established concerns employing white-
     collar middle-class reverse commuters must
     make special arrangements to assure their
     labor supply. The Reader's Digest, for exam-
     ple, moved from downtown Manhattan to Chap-
     paqua in northern Westchester in 1923, and
     in 1969 it still had a chartered bus meeting
     the train from New York to shuttle women to
     the plant.

The conclusion of the Tri-State Transportation
Commission study places the City and regional picture
in a careful perspective. It deserves quoting almost
in its entirety.

In analyzing mass transit usage by the
low, middle, and high income groups,
homesites and worksites were classified
with respect to location within or outside of New York City. For New York City
residents there is a clear tendency to-
wards declining transit patronage as
household income increases, regardless
of work location. In addition, transit
usage for residents employed within the
city is about twice that for residents
working outside the City regardless of
income, reflecting in part the service,
coverage, and orientation of the New York
City transit system.

For residents outside New York City,
the use of transit by those employed in
New York City is fairly constant at around
50 per cent. But for those both residing
and working outside the city, transit
usage varies from 20 per cent for the low
income group to under 5 per cent for those
in the highest income category.

The dependence of low income households on mass transit facilities demonstrates a somewhat obvious, but important
point. In view of the low auto availability rates among low income households
it seems clear that an investment in
transportation directed specifically at
improving accessibility to employment
opportunities must be limited to the area
of mass transportation. It appears that
the presence of an efficient highway system, while otherwise desirable, is not
sufficient in providing improved transportation capabilities for the poor.[3]

LOS ANGELES

In July, 1966, a mass transportation demonstration
project, eventually involving an outlay of $2.7 million,
began in the south-central and East Los Angeles area to
test the assumption that increased public transportation can substantially improve employment opportunities
for the residents of a disadvantaged area. The project

covered an area of forty-six square miles and included a population of half a million people. The majority of the working residents had incomes below the poverty level, and the gross rate of unemployment was
about three times that of the Los Angeles metropolitan
area as a whole.

Work on the project was divided into three
phases: (a) An operational test of a bus service in
the poverty area; (b) Studies of public transportation
needs of the project area; and (c) A limited number of
operational tests of the conclusions reached by the
studies in the second phase.

Four progress reports have been prepared, and
deficiencies in public transportation in the area have
been recorded.   These include:[4]

(1)   Lack of transfer privileges between lines of
       the Southern California Rapid Transit Dis-
       trict and the six other private and munici-
       pal bus operators serving the project area.

(2)   Lack of transfer privileges between the
       Southern California Rapid Transit District
       and suburban lines.

(3)   Lack of an adequate grid system of public
       transportation routes to serve the widely
       dispersed industrial and commercial areas.

A number of recommendations were made to test
these conclusions. Significantly, it was noted that
the industrial areas that were proposed to be served
were so isolated and difficult to reach by existing
public transportation that it was improbable that
there were any residents of the poverty area traveling
to or from these areas by bus. Accordingly, the recommended bus services were designed to provide low-
cost transportation from the project area to places o:
employment that could not readily be reached by existing public transportation.

The initial bus service is known as the Century
Boulevard Line Number 100. Within a year after inau-
guration, traffic on this line reached 2,600 riders
per day; monthly revenues of $15,000 were covering
more than 38 per cent of total expenses of operation.
Surveys revealed that 78 per cent of all passengers
were new riders who had not previously made the trip

by bus. Of those who indicated trip purpose, nearly
59 per cent were traveling to or from work and 20 per
cent were on school trips. On the other hand, only 25
per cent (220 passengers) of the work-trip passengers
could properly be classed as project area residents
who were assisted in obtaining employment through the
new service (survey of March 2, 1967). Later surveys
(January, 1968) showed that the improvement in transportation contributed only marginally to improvements
in employment. An intensive employment drive in the
area nearby linked to job sites revealed that over
four fifths of the new job applicants could not even
be referred to jobs, as their level of skills was far
below what was required.

The contract subsidy for this service was scheduled to expire July 1, 1968, by which time average
weekday traffic was expected to reach 3,000 passengers
and the revenue per mile to be approximately 40 cents,
estimated to cover about 70 per cent of out-of-pocket
cost of operation. As the line continues its operation, the development of riding habits and the development of new job information flows are bringing about
increase in use by new workers.

One of the interesting by-products of this project to date has been the extension of the transit
information program. It was recognized that underuse
or inefficient use of existing public transportation
in the project area was due also to lack of knowledge
of the routes. The nature of the problem was well
summarized:[5]

> The Los Angeles metropolitan area with
> its widely scattered development requires
> an unusually extensive and complex public
> transportation system to serve its resi-
> dents and activities. With such a decen-
> tralized pattern, a traveller must become
> familiar with about as many different
> destinations and route combinations as
> his number of activities.
>
> Migration and relocation character-
> istics of people result in a great lack
> of familiarity with the geography, making
> it difficult for them to recognize and
> consider alternative ways of reaching
> destinations.

In order to overcome deficiencies in public
transportation due primarily to a lack of information,
a map was prepared, showing all local and interurban
public transportation routes in the Los Angeles area.
The maps were displayed at information centers throughout the project area. Information centers are also
being established in churches, schools, public agency
offices, and at private employment and welfare agencies and other facilities that are in contact with
slum-area residents.

The main features of the map are the distinction
between local and suburban services and between radial
and crosstown lines; the indication of frequency of
service on individual routes by use of varying line
widths; and the location of parks, colleges and high
schools, hospitals, industrial areas, and other points
of interest.

The utility of this map for job placements was
clearly noted:[6]

> The manually prepared versions of this
> map, which have been in use since November,
> 1966, have been valuable aids to the per-
> sonnel of several agencies in their re-
> ferral of persons to jobs and services.
> Widespread use of the new map, in con-
> junction with timetables will substan-
> tially increase the ability of counselors
> or individuals to select the most effi-
> cient and least expensive route combinations
> for reaching destinations.

Another important part of the information program
involves timetables. New timetables include a map
that for the first time shows connections with the
Century Boulevard line and other routes of the Southern California Rapid Transit District. Extensive
distribution of these timetables increased the usage
of both the Century Boulevard line and of other lines.

In addition to these information aids, a special
summer project utilized manpower available through the
Neighborhood Youth Corps and STEP, Inc., in coopera-
tion with the Watts-Compton Improvement Association,
to provide information on public transportation to
persons in the project area who are not reached by
other means.

The key to this particular <u>ad hoc</u> approach is the availability of young persons who live in the community and who can be trained to understand, transmit, and discuss information on public transportation with their neighbors. After completing a brief period of training, these "Information Aides," distribute timetables, maps, and other descriptive literature and explain to residents how they may use available bus services to meet their daily needs. The aides record complaints, comments, or suggestions from those they contact.

In answer to complaints that beaches and other recreational facilities were inaccessible to project-area youths who do not own cars, it was decided to provide information on existing public transportation to places of recreation as well as employment. A sixteen-page booklet entitled "You Can Go Places This Summer," showing points of recreation and how to get there by bus, was prepared and 65,000 copies were distributed to junior and senior high-school students in the project area. Another 1,000 additional copies were distributed through youth agencies in the project area and 9,000 copies will be distributed in three versions: one for the Florence-Watts-Willowbrook area, one for the Avalon-Exposition area, and one for East Los Angeles. The primary differences between the editions occur in the pages on which "Close-to-Home" recreational facilities such as parks, swimming pools, and activities in each subarea are listed. Where different routes would be required to reach major recreational or cultural facilities from the different areas, the maps were altered.[7]

The Watts experiment, while not a full test of the precise extent to which employment of slum residents can be increased through better transportation links, shows that employment does increase as transportation difficulties are removed. Furthermore, unlike the situation in New York City, it shows also how the general social isolation of slum areas can be reduced by adjusting transit services to the peculiar needs of these communities.

SUBURBAN TRANSPORTATION EXPERIMENTS

The Urban Mass Transportation Act of 1964 provided the Federal Housing and Urban Development Department with the authority and the funds for a number of grants

designed to help provide transportation to low-income
groups so that they may take advantage of available
employment and other income opportunities outside
their communities. Since 1965, more than $200 million
in federal grants have been made available to more
than twenty-seven states for improvement in services
to public service systems.

While not all of these funds were allocated to
projects primarily aimed at the low-income population,
a large number were. Philadelphia, Minneapolis, Dallas
St.Louis, Chicago, Cleveland, Norfolk, Buffalo, and
Wilmington have projects being planned, developed, or
implemented; in each case the goal is to improve the
transportation service so that low-income groups can
take advantage of employment opportunities outside
the CBD.

In March, 1967, the Department of Housing and
Urban Development announced a poverty-area bus demonstration project in Nassau County, New York. The purpose of the $2.2 million grant was to provide job
accessibility to low-income residents of Nassau and
Suffolk counties.

Nassau and Suffolk counties, with a combined population of 2.3 million, include numerous pockets of
poverty with a relatively high rate of unemployment
scattered among the communities. There are about
fifty-three relatively large industrial parks with an
estimated employment of 150,000 and with a severe
shortage of semiskilled and unskilled workers. Located away from residential concentrations and traditional radial patterns of transportation, the
industries can be reached only be automobile or by
complicated bus routes. The number of job openings
that have remained unfilled because of lack of transportation has been estimated as high as 5,000. In
addition to industrial parks, there are numerous
hospitals in the area which are often understaffed.

Service was instituted on three routes in July,
1967, under the direction of the New York State Office
of Transportation and administered by the Tri-State
Transportation Commission. Two of the routes involve
direct bus service from Hempstead in central Nassau
County, and from Bar Harbour in southeastern Nassau
County, to Engineer's Hill Industrial Park in Plain-
view, Nassau County, eliminating a substantial number
of transfers formerly required to make these trips.

A third route (to within two blocks of all firms in the industrial park) is from Hicksville transportation center, which connects with eleven bus routes and the Long Island Rail Road, which will increase its service from three trips to fourteen trips daily.[8]

The project is scheduled through three phases.

Phase I involves a twelve-month test, with option for a twelve-month extension, of a regularly scheduled, conventional-type bus service to ascertain whether such a service can improve employment opportunities among unskilled and semiskilled workers.

Phase II involves detailed studies of the location and availability of labor supply, the location of non-CBD employment concentrations throughout Long Island (Nassau and Suffolk Counties), the adequacy of existing transit services in terms of needs, and how existing services can be restructured or supplemented to eliminate specifically identified deficiencies.

Phase III involves the provision and testing of specific transportation services designed to eliminate deficiencies identified during Phase II. Funds for this phase will be released, within the over-all project budget and with the concurrence of HUD, upon the development of specific and detailed action programs.

Among the recommendations to be considered are such things as changes in schedules, routing, fares, transfer privileges (with the buses to tap poverty areas on Long Island and with the railroad to tap poverty areas in New York City), public information techniques, and special contractural-type bus services.[9]

By August, 1967, ridership had reached 9,044 and revenue amounted to $2,502, representing 36.5 per cent of the project's bus operating costs. Work-oriented trips comprised 47 per cent of total ridership; 25 per cent of these trips represented apparently new jobs, as the respondents stated that they did not make the trip prior to inauguration of the service.

Whether, indeed, the Nassau experiment is a success is not yet clear. It has been reported that some

users have said that they could not hold their new
jobs without the bus, even with its fare of eighty
cents a day. There are also indications, from employers, that part-time employment has increased. On
the other hand, residents of the slum ghettos who have
to take another bus to reach the experimental loop
service find that the high cost prohibits commuting.
Given hourly rates for unskilled work of between $1.50
and $1.80, a commutation cost of $10 a week indicates
a problem of the type and dimension that the Project
Labor Market study had identified in the City.[10]

Like the Watts experiment, the Nassau experiment
shows that the transportation barrier to employment
can be reduced by pinpointed and careful planning.

NOTES

1. Tri-State Transportation Commission, <u>Trans-
portation, the Link Between People and Jobs</u> (Interim
Technical Report 4088-6051-6556, June, 1968). (Mimeo-
graphed.)

2. <u>Ibid</u>., p. 20.

3. <u>Ibid</u>., p. 42.

4. <u>South Central and East Los Angeles Transpor-
tation-Employment Project</u>, Progress Report No. 4
(July, 1967).

5. <u>Ibid</u>., p. 28.

6. <u>Ibid</u>., p. 30.

7. <u>Ibid</u>., p. 31.

8. <u>HUD News</u>, No. 1380, U.S. Department of Housing and Urban Development (Friday, March 17, 1967),
p. 1.

9. <u>Ibid</u>., p. 3.

10. <u>The New York Times</u> (September 10, 1967),
p. 63.

CHAPTER **7** APPROACHES TO
SOLUTIONS

Linking homesites with work sites will continue
to be a problem of urban societies. Neither decentralization nor decreases in the size of production
and service units can be expected in the future.
Changing tastes, and a technology evolving more rapidly in fields other than housing, seem to assure that
future job sites--on the average--will continue to
shift more rapidly than residential locations. Regardless of future population or product growth rates--
and regardless of poverty standards--one can be sure
that in the future those in the lower portions of the
income distribution will be more handicapped in going
to work than they are now.

Strategies meant to reduce the poor's handicap
in going to work are particular to each city. A set
of specific proposals for New York has been put forth;
we have also seen how other cities have tried to cope
with their problems. Here, because the problem is so
general, one must search for broad categories of solutions. These, of necessity, must center on the question of why the public transportation network is so
generally lagging behind the cities' changes in employment and residential locations.

In the economists' "long-run analysis" the problem is trivial; it involves the allocation of human
resources only in the most marginal sense. Indeed,
the poor's transportation handicap cannot be seen as
creating a major bottleneck in manpower availability
in terms of the nation's total productive effort.
Yet in the short run the labor market does not work;
witness the persistence of the unemployed poor in the
core cities' slums alongside unfilled low-skill job
vacancies throughout the city and suburbs. From the
worker's point of view the market does not work
either; witness the permanence over the years of the
travel-to-work handicap of the large city poor.

The low level of job accessibility to the poor
is part of that configuration of problems referred to
in the phrase "the plight of the city." At the heart
of this plight--underlying the cities' fiscal stress--
are lagging social values, broad inefficiencies in the
allocation of resources, and gaps and failures in
planning. In The Affluent Society, J. K. Galbraith
suggests that there is very little likelihood that
the quality of the urban environment will improve
without major shifts in social values.[1] In The New
Industrial State, Professor Galbraith deals at length
with the anomaly of effective and continuous planning
in the private sector (where the myth has it that market reigns and planning is anathema) and the public
sector (where the opposite is supposed to hold). He
points to urban and interurban transportation as the
major example of a lack of planning.[2]

Nationally, these planning lacunae stem from
multiple private ownership of bus and railroad companies, diverse administrative jurisdictions, and the
lack of effective centralized planning mechanisms.
Yet one must note that in the large metropolitan areas,
urban mass transportation systems are public and
quasi-public, and well-staffed transportation authori-
ties do much planning. In the typical large metropolitan area there are in fact many--often a dozen or
more--planning agencies; in addition, federal policy
generally requires at least one of these agencies to
plan for transportation for the entire metropolitan
area. There are planning failures as well as lacunae.
Here we are concerned primarily with the former. The
specific question of this study is why routes do not
serve the poor--not the more general problem of the
level and quality of urban transportation.[3] The real
question is why we plan so poorly in bringing workers
and jobs together.

No matter how much one might wish to find examples of an evil conspiracy, delving into the history
of specific routing decisions does not yield even
hints of systemic decision-making meant to handicap
the poor. Various social analyses based on some form
of deliberate worker exploitation do not hold water.
On the contrary, one is led to the conclusion that
employers--private or public--would stand to benefit
were workers to appear at their gates in greater num-
bers.

There being no basic vested interest opposing
them, there is every presumption that remedial strategies linking homesites and work sites can be applied.

As indicated earlier, the proposed solution for
New York stemmed in part from the finding that the
city's transportation system is a well-developed one.
The solution is not a general one, nor did our study
come to grips with the fundamental issues of pricing
and investment. Such questions go beyond the scope
of this study. This chapter has more limited goals:
to set forth, in broad terms, the threshold requirements of a general planning strategy to improve the
poor's accessibility to job sites, to review some of
the project solutions, and to isolate a set of broadly
applicable remedial strategies.

NEED FOR A REORIENTATION
IN TRANSPORTATION PLANNING

In transportation, planning is the central fact.
One doesn't need to advocate it. Whether publicly or
privately run, transportation comes into being only
after elaborate plans have been developed. This is
true of automobiles or airplanes, interurban or intraurban transportation. To plan or not to plan is not
the issue. The issues are who does the planning and
how and for whom is it done? Should planning be
national, regional, metropolitan, or urban in scope?
Should planning be responsive primarily to pressures
from the demand side, or from the supply side? If the
former, routes will be determined primarily by land-
use patterns: If the latter, transportation will be
provided primarily by an excessively capital-intensive
technology.

Most recent analyses on how best to balance supply
and demand requirements and decisions have dealt with
administrative problems and local governmental reorganization. The prognosis for rapid changes in this
area is rather dismal. Furthermore, the ultimate
rationale for a single agency making regional transportation policy--the solution advocated most frequent-
ly[4]--is heavily anchored in the accepted dictum that
"the control of transport facilities is the most
powerful means to the town planner to bring about a
desired pattern of land use,"[5] This indicates that

linking job sites with the residential locations of
the poor is a matter for the more distant future.

Given the fact of current structural difficulties
in transportation planning, we focus here on less
global proposals for restructuring the transportation
planning processes. The proposed restructuring does
not deal with all of the many aspects of the urban
transportation conundrum; it focuses on the problem
of travel to work. It is hoped that the proposed solutions of this problem are consistent with broader
solutions.

The first requirement is a reorientation of the
attitudes of those concerned with urban transportation.
Transportation planning is the province of the tech-
nologist. Planning agencies generally are staffed by
able engineers and frustrated train buffs. The staff's
drive for achievement and the high cost of the equipment involved lead to a high commitment to "the newest
in technology" and to a search for the latest industrial product. Much attention, for example, is given
to the possibility of introducing pneumatic trains
that would run in underground steel tubes from which
the air is evacuated by huge electric pumps.[6] The New
York Metropolitan Transportation Authority proudly
reported in September, 1968, that it had set up an integrated computerized model on which it was simulating
different subway speeds, frequencies, loads, etc.
Meanwhile, the authority's buses run on the same routes
as the horse-drawn trolleys of 1908.

The focus on heavy durable equipment with the
large sunken costs involved necessarily demands careful planning. Making heavy fixed investments in the
face of rapid technological and social change is a
very risky matter. A wrong guess will be very expen-
sive. To maintain social and to avoid personal ac-
countability, the planning process involves overlays
of administrative agencies and much public and private
debate. The planning cycle lengthens while conditions
change. Yet once the planning cycle is started, the
plan's fundamental character can rarely be changed.
An extreme example of the result of the complexities of
of the planning mechanism is two spurs to the New York
City subway system put into operation early in 1968
along plans developed in 1940. Another example, for
New York City, can be found in the proposed Second
Avenue subway that has been in the planning stage for
more than six years. Very long lags between the

identification of travel needs--itself not an easy
matter--and the provision of services are thus guaran-
teed.

Urban planning institutions must be reorganized
to be more responsive to the rapidity of social
changes. Concern with service must balance concern
with equipment; the technologically appropriate must
be put ahead of the technologically advanced.

The second requirement for the development of
remedial strategies is the availability of more data
about travel, and particularly about intraurban travel
patterns. Most information on travel-to-work patterns
is census-based, and thus intermittent and too aggre-
gative. Until recently, supplementary survey-based
data were available only rarely, for limited purposes,
and in a few very large metropolitan centers. To
plead for more data is easy; obtaining them is costly.
Yet, the availability of more and better data is a
major prerequisite.

Recasting and reanalyzing available data is the
next best thing to the development of original data.
Station toll counts on subways and visual traffic
counts on buses (used currently to determine frequencies of service) can often identify changes in the
travel patterns of the poor, when linked to the socio-
economic characteristics of the areas where the counts
are taken. Analyses of the impact of transportation
strikes have long underlined the poor's greater dependence on public transportation. Coupled with variations in establishment absenteeism statistics, such
strike impact data also can throw light on the poor's
travel-to-work patterns.

The third requirement for the development of
remedial strategies is greater participation in transportation planning by the general public and by slum
residents. The technological orientation and the accounting complexities of urban planning operations
have made them primarily a matter of and for special-
ists. Representatives of the general public, even
when inclined to do so, find it difficult to intervene. When public interventions occur, they take
place through a variety of watchdog "Citizens Budget
Commissions," generally representing the interests of
businessmen and real-estate speculators. The active
politician and the legislator are also limited in
their power to intervene. The partial autonomy of

of most transportation planning agencies, the rules
of the political game, and the intricacy of the issue
all conspire to encourage restraint.

That political intervention in transportation is
to be avoided is part of conventional wisdom. That--
on the contrary--it may be very effective is exempli-
fied in the recent launching of a campaign in a county
on Long Island to alter the helter-skelter pattern of
bus routes. The County Executive refused to renew
franchises. The private bus companies at first fought
back but finally agreed to extend their routes and
eliminate transfers; provide more convenient and
timely service to Long Island Rail Road stations; co-
ordinate transfer points and connections with other
bus lines; furnish special service to universities,
hospitals, and courts; and install reduced fares for
children, older persons, and poverty groups. The use
of franchising powers thus achieved what the transportation planning commission should have been concerned with but was not--and what it probably could
not have achieved if it had tried.

The value of political intervention by community-
based agencies and a newly aroused general public was
shown also by the 1969 debates on the routes to be
followed by the planned Second Avenue subway in New
York City. Here, the plan originally submitted by the
technicians of the transportation agencies contemplated
a straight north-south run along the well-developed
avenue. The plan ignored the Lower East Side bulge,
which is comprised primarily of poor residences and
small manufacturers. Public clamor at the hearings
led to a redesign of the proposed line to bring it
somewhat closer to the residences of the poor.

Political action and participation of slum residents in such complicated matters must be viewed with
care. Surely the general experience with participation in community action agencies has been far from
encouraging. Indeed, it has been said by at least one
author to have made for maximum feasible misunder-
standing. Yet the experience of recent pilot projects
indicates that increased use of the new lines is related to the introduction of "transportation aides"
able to convey to the poor the new service availability and able to interpret to the transportation
agency the needs of the poor.[7] Participation of the
poor on transportation planning boards should cer-
tainly help to identify their travel patterns and needs.

ALTERNATIVE PROPOSALS

The new awareness of urban poverty, of ghetto
misery, and of the difficulties the poor have in
traveling to work has spawned numerous proposals for
solution of these problems. Few of these programs
have much merit. More often than not, their limited
merit does not stem from inherently faulty analysis
or errors of techniques but rather from the fact that
small advances in central city reorganization of services are often Pyrrhic victories.

The problems of the ghetto, for instance, will
not be solved by much less than complete changes in
land-use patterns, a more rapid rate of low-income
housing development, and the reduction of segregation
throughout the metropolis. Skills for the urban poor
demand fundamental changes in the way they are provided, etc. Nor can one argue a priori that improved
transportation to work is all that is needed. It is
impossible to establish scientifically whether improved transportation is more or less important than
better distribution of information about job openings
and active employer recruitment efforts to match potential employees to potential jobs. All evidence
points, contrary to popular belief, to active job-
hunting patterns by the poor.[8]

Improvements in transportation are clearly a
good place to start in reducing the structural inefficiencies that abound in the labor market. Social
change being marginal, and partial solutions being
more amenable to implementation than total ones, the
latter must be given priority. A minimal requirement
of partial solutions is that what is to be done must
not run contrary to long-run requirements, realities,
and goals.

Some of the proposals geared to reducing the
level of unemployment of the slums point to the importance of self-contained ghetto economic development. This has much appeal and obvious immediate
politico-social gains. Yet, even if successful,
ghetto economic development will make a small dent in
the unemployment of the poor. Jobs continue to move
to the outer suburbs at an increasing rate. Ghetto
economic development will not create many new vacancies, and, anyway, gilding the ghetto is contrary to
the trends of "scatteration" of the poor throughout
the metropolis and the major social goal of residential
desegregation.

To concentrate on the issue of bringing the poor
to shifting job sites, we will deal primarily with
proposals that (1) aim at providing the poor with
automobiles, or their equivalent, and (2) suggest that
the poor be provided with free transportation.

Cars for the Poor

Taking a leaf from the name and early advertising
campaigns for the Volkswagen and costing out all aspects, Sumner Myers recently concluded that "the VW
owner, carrying one other worker at $1 per day, and
the used car owner carrying two would just about break
even with using the bus." From this Myers argues for
some kind of program designed to provide the poor with
cars through an organization geared to "donate the use
of a car to any underemployed person who wishes to
look for a better paying job."[9]

It is refreshing to find social scientists who
take seriously the politician's slogan "a chicken in
every pot and a car in every garage" because of the
new emphasis on the word "every." The proposal has
limited possibilities and many drawbacks. Clearly,
as its proponent claims, "it's worth a try!" It is
in line with current social values, fulfills the
middle-class aspirations of the poor, and may become
an incentive to the young to find jobs and hold them.
Myers argues that the proposal has an important value
because "it brings the poor into the mainstream of the
rest of society--even if that stream is clogged with
traffic!"[10] Surely in this sense it militates against
the long-term requirements of metropolitan reorganization.

A related proposal is the provision of taxilike
services, the cost of which is cut by the sharing of
rides. Fundamentally what is involved is a "dial-a-
bus" service with centralized computerized dispatching
and complete or almost complete door-to-door linking
of home and job. The cost of such a system has been
worked out at roughly 50 per cent more than the per-
mile cost of operating a private car but at one fourth
the cost of a taxi. The system has other advantages:

> The service flexibility of a taxi-bus
> system also calls for pricing flexibility
> which can be used to favor the poor. For
> example, by charging lower fares for
> trips which either begin or end in a

poverty zone, the poor may be subsidized
without a "means" test and without subsidizing everybody else who uses what we
hope will be a very high-quality system.[11]

The theory of the "dial-a-bus" system has been
worked out in sufficient detail to assume that tech-
nically it will work and, clearly, it will enlarge the
job opportunity potential of the poor. The difficulty
appears to be that at least some of the nonpoor must
participate in the system for it to be effective. All
studies of urban residential and travel patterns under-
line the extent to which the maintaining of "social
distance" ranks high in the preferences of middle-
class individuals; thus, the problem may be serious.

Both forms of the "cars for the poor" proposals
seem to depend upon the establishment of new organiza-
tions even with the difficulties inherent in such
ventures.

Free Fares in
Public Transportation

Starting from the recognition that one of the
major causes of the urban traffic problem is the imbalance between the price of a private car ride and
the price of a bus fare, a number of students of urban
transportation argued as early as 1959 for free bus
fares or their equivalent as the way to straighten out
the imbalance.[12] In 1967, the U.S. Department of
Transportation revived this idea, applied it to the
problems of poverty and job decentralization, and
coupled it with concern for the decline in use of mass
urban public transportation. Indeed, the cost of bus
transport, while relatively high for those who have an
alternative in the automobile, is higher yet for the
underemployed who may have to trade off transportation
with subsistence necessities.

Proposed schemes for providing free transportation on buses were analyzed, as to feasibility, by
Charles River Associates of Cambridge, Massachusetts.
The study found that a free transit program appeared
to be "a costly and largely ineffective means" of providing slum residents with access to job areas.[13]
The detailed feasibility analysis showed that the poor
do not gain by going freely to places where there is
no reason for them to go. Indeed, Charles River Associates found the basic problem to be that "the transit

system often provides reasonable service only for the
radial trip pattern that was predominant several de-
cades ago rather than for the cross-city trips which
are now needed to move ghetto residents to dispersed
job opportunities."[14] Thus the stress was once again
upon improvement of the existing plant--more crosstown lines and increased geographic coverage.

Partial alternatives to providing free transportation have long existed in many cities. These mainly
involve subsidizing special groups such as the aged
and elementary and high-school students. There has
never been any scientific evaluation of the impact of
such subsidies; it is possible that they are truly
helpful because the transport requirements of these
groups appear well served by existing routes.

Rerouting of
Transportation Networks

Updating information about the travel needs of
the poor and adjusting existing bus routes to shifts
in job sites are the most common remedial recommendations of the surveys recently conducted in various
cities. Our proposal for bus rerouting in New York
City thus belongs to a pattern of remedial strategies
that appear to have large acceptance.

The advantages of the rerouting approach are many:
(1) It calls for very limited actual outlays; more
often than not, all that is involved is the shifting
of administrative focus and corollary bookkeeping
costs.   (2)   It calls for reversible decisions and no
investment in fixed plant. All that is required is a
willingness by the urban planners to experiment and
to wait long enough to see whether the experiment is
worthwhile.   (3)   Increased information about bus
routes and the transportation network involves small
costs and assured, even if not easily traceable, benefits to various population groups.   (4)   Bus rerouting
incurs little if any opposition, as it does not necessarily call for decreasing CBD-oriented services.

There is no major logical disadvantage to experimentation with rerouting. The skeptic might note that
most newly established bus lines to get ghetto residents to jobs carry relatively few passengers. Measured by load factors--the traditional measure of
average to "peak" volume--the experiments might even
appear to be failures. Such an analysis is in error

on several counts: (1) Availability of access to the
place of employment does not in itself either create a
flow of labor to the employer's gate or guarantee that
the employer hires from the new labor supply.   (2)
While the employer has vacancies, he does not fill them
overnight.   (3) Transit habits do not get established
overnight.   More fundamental, in most analyses that
argue that experimental lines are failures, is the fact
that measures of bus utilization are compared with
average load factors for the city.   The comparison is
erroneous.   Experimental bus route load factors must
be matched against the work trip component of the load
factor.   For most cities this is less than half the
average city load factors.[15]   When so measured, experimental buses carry about as many passengers to work
as do the bus lines not experimenting with new routes.

In a broader sense bus rerouting proposals are
consistent with the results of larger analytical efforts connected with job creation for the poor.   They
avoid errors associated with exclusively ghetto-based
programs that are likely to be counterproductive.   The
bus rerouting approach is fundamentally in line with
other efforts at accelerating the pace of development
in growing metropolitan areas that have been proved
the quickest and cheapest methods for over-all economic improvement.

Alfred Marshall's discussion on poverty--written
in 1890--begins on the note that "prompt action is
needed in regard to the large, though it may be hoped,
now steadily diminishing, 'residuum' of persons who
are incapable of doing a good day's work with which
to earn a good day's wage."[16]   The call, unfortunately,
is still apt; now is the time for prompt action.

NOTES

1.   J. K. Galbraith, The Affluent Society (New
York: Mentor Books, 1958), pp. 240-49.

2.   J. K. Galbraith, The New Industrial State
(Boston: Houghton Mifflin Co., 1967), pp. 356-57.

3.   The over-all problem of level and quality of
transportation is obviously linked with that of routes.
See, for example, W. R. Thompson, A Preface to Urban

<u>Economics</u> (Baltimore: The Johns Hopkins Press, 1965),
pp. 333-60.

4. See, for example, J. A. Bailey, <u>Urban Trans-
portation</u>, a paper presented at the Conference of the
American Society for Public Administration (Miami,
1969).

5. See, for example, S. P. C. Plouden, "Transportation Studies Examined," <u>Journal of Transport Economics and Policy</u> (January, 1967), p. 13.

6. The romance with heavy technology in trans-
portation--appropriate for interurban movement--
spreads to groups associated with transportation-
operating agencies, as with the pneumatic train proposal for the New York Regional Plan Association. See
N.Y.R.P.A., <u>The Regional Plan</u> (November, 1968).

7. See the Watts experiment, Chapter 6 of this
volume.

8. H. L. Sheppard and A. H. Belitsky, <u>The Job
Hunt</u> (Baltimore: The Johns Hopkins Press, 1966).

9. S. Myers, "Personal Transportation for the
Poor," a paper presented at the Conference on Poverty
and Transportation, American Academy of Arts and Sci-
ences (Boston, June, 1968).

10. S. Myers, "Looking Ahead," <u>National Planning
Association Bulletin</u> (September, 1968), p. 6.

11. <u>Ibid</u>.

12. L. L. Waters, "Free Transit: A Way Out of
Traffic Jams," <u>Business Horizons</u> (Indiana School of
Business, Spring, 1959).

13. Charles River Associates, <u>An Evaluation of
Free Transit Service</u> (Cambridge, August, 1968).

14. <u>Ibid</u>.

15. See, for example, Chicago Area Transportation
Study, <u>Survey of Findings</u> (Chicago, 1959).

16. Alfred Marshall, <u>Principles of Economics</u>, all
editions, Vol. VI (New York: Macmillan), Sec. 12.

APPENDIXES

APPENDIX A

DEFINITION AND LOCATION OF
POVERTY AREAS IN NEW YORK CITY

APPENDIX A

The areas included in this study were defined as concentrations of first-magnitude poverty as shown in terms of health areas. These areas were identified in a study completed on May 1, 1966, by the City Administrator's office with assistance from the City Planning, Health and Welfare Departments; the Youth Board; and the Economic Opportunity Committee.

The City Administrator's study based its recommendations on an analysis of the comparative rates of persons receiving welfare, welfare recipients over age sixty-five, welfare recipients under age eighteen, juvenile deliquency, live births, out-of-wedlock live births, venereal disease, infant mortality, and family income under $4,000 per year. The poverty health areas were identified by giving intensity weights to three of these indexes--total persons receiving welfare, juvenile delinquency, and live births--which were found to reflect other measures.

The following areas were shown to be first-magnitude poverty areas:

Manhattan: Central Harlem
            East Harlem
            Lower East Side

Bronx: Crotona Park-East Tremont
        South Bronx (Morrisania)

Brooklyn: Williamsburg
           Bedford-Stuyvesant
           Brownsville and East New York
           Coney Island

Queens: South Jamaica

A complete listing of health areas and the census tracts contained therein for these poverty areas will be found at the end of Appendix A.

The 1960 Census of Population provides detailed demographic data for each census tract contained in New York City's health areas. Analysis of these data for poverty areas, compared with similar data for selected middle-income areas and averages for the five boroughs and the total City of New York, provides a quantified perspective for the examination of transportation requirements of poverty-area residents.

For the purpose of an analysis of census data, the poverty areas have been grouped as follows:

Harlem
Lower East Side
East Tremont
South Bronx
Brooklyn Analysis Area A
Brooklyn Analysis Area B
Brooklyn Analysis Area C
Brooklyn Analysis Area D
Brooklyn Analysis Area E*
South Jamaica

For purposes of comparison and control, two middle-income neighborhoods were selected in Queens:

Flushing
Richmond Hill

---

*Although Coney Island is classified as a first-magnitude poverty area, it was excluded from most of the Brooklyn analysis because of the diverse economic and social character of the area. Seagate, an isolated middle-class community, contrasts markedly with the adjacent Thirty-seventh Street-Stillwell Avenue neighborhood. Aggregations of census data for the entire area are of little value. (See The New York Times, July 24, 1967.)

Appendix Figure I

MAP OF CENTRAL BROOKLYN ANALYSIS AREAS

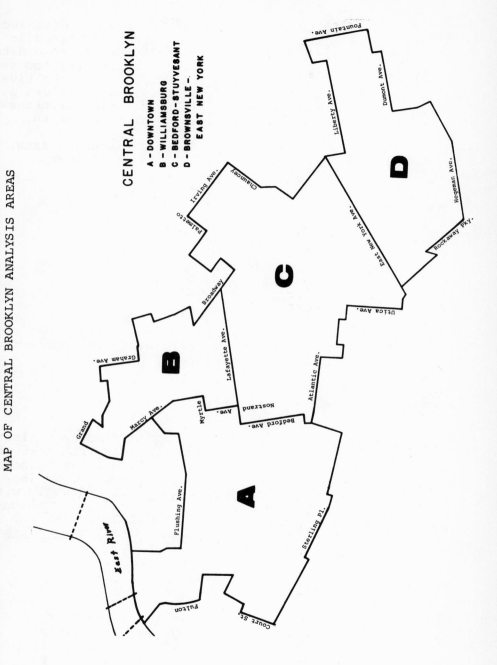

CENTRAL BROOKLYN

A – DOWNTOWN
B – WILLIAMSBURG
C – BEDFORD–STUYVESANT
D – BROWNSVILLE –
    EAST NEW YORK

LIST OF CENSUS TRACTS INCLUDED
IN POVERTY HEALTH AREAS

	Health Area	Census Tracts
Bronx	18	231,375.0,165
	20	363,365,367
	21.10	361,359,161
	21.20	155,157
	26	149,147,145
	27	151,153
	28	131,125
	29	119,121,123
	34	143,141,139
	35	137,135,133
	36	129,127
	37	87,89
Bronx	39	67,69
	40	71,75,77
	41	73,79,35,31
	42	83,85
	44	37,33,43
	45	41,39,23,25
	47	17,15,11,13
	24	167,169,163
Brooklyn	6	523,525,527,529
	10	13,21,25,23
	11	27,29.0,29.1,31,185.0,185.1
	12	33,35,181,183,187,195,197
	13	193,201,227,229,231,233
	14	189,191,235,237,239,241,255
	15	487,489,491,505,507,509,511
	17	257,259,285.0,285.1,389,391
	18	253,259.0,261
	19	281,283,287,289
	20	251,263,265,277,275
	21	279,291,293,387
	24	27,41,43,69,71
	26	39,127,129.0,129.1,161,163
	27.10	179,199,203,205,223,225
	28	243,245,247,249,267,269,271.0
	30	273,295,297,381,385,383
	31	371,375,373,377,379

	Health Areas	Census Tracts
Brooklyn (cont.)	34	397,399,415,417,419,435
	35	401,403,409,411,413,437
	36	271.1,299,301,309,311
	37	365.0,365.1,367,369
Brooklyn	50.20	347,349,357,359,361,363
	56	900,902
	57	904,906,908,1136,1138
	59	910,912, 914, 1134
	60	916,918,920
	61	1152,1154,1156,1158,1160
	62	1150,1162,1164,1166,1192,1194
	63	1126,1128,1130,1132
	90.10	328,330,336,340,342
	90.20	326,348.0,348.1,350,354,356,352
	52	307,303
	58.20	892,894,896,898
Manhattan	7.20	231,0,227.0
	8	243.1,236,234,232,214
	10	230,228
	11	219,217.0,213.0
	12	224,226
	13	212,208
	15	222,220,200
	16	196,198,204,206,210
	17	192,194,202
	85.10	221.1,227.1,231.1,235.1
	19	190,218
	20	182,184
	21	178,180,188
	24	186,216
	85.20	217.1,213.1,209.1,207.1,201.1, 197.1
	23.20	197.0,193
	25	172,174
	26	162,164,170
	28.10	166,168
	32.10	181,185,189
Manhattan	63	24,28
	67	26
Queens	34	246,248,250,252,258,260,262, 264,266,270,272,274,276,278, 280,282,284,288,290

APPENDIX B

STATISTICAL APPENDIX

CENSUS DATA FOR NEW YORK CITY RESIDENTS,
POVERTY AREAS AND SELECTED MIDDLE-INCOME AREAS

	% of Families Income Under $4,000	% of Workers Using Public Trans.	% of Households with Auto Available	% of Workers Who Walk to Work	% of Population Nonwhite	% Male Unemployed (Civ.Lab.F.)	Per Cent of Households		
							Same House as 1955	Different House Outside SMSA	Different House in City
Harlem	51.6	76.1	14.7	6.8	66.3	7.9	58.7	3.9	30.9
Lower East Side	50.3	75.0	12.9	9.1	10.6	9.5	52.9	1.9	34.7
East Tremont	45.2	68.6	21.5	9.2	38.6	8.1	52.5	3.0	33.4
South Bronx	41.3	72.5	20.8	8.0	23.0	7.7	51.9	2.1	35.2
Brooklyn – A	42.2	66.5	22.6	12.0	41.9	7.7	46.3	4.6	36.7
" B	45.9	66.3	22.8	13.8	27.2	8.7	44.7	2.5	40.9
" C	38.1	70.2	30.4	6.5	60.6	6.8	52.4	4.7	33.3
" D	40.3	64.9	30.4	11.9	21.2	7.3	51.8	2.4	39.9
" E	40.5	60.8	34.2	9.9	7.5	7.1	56.7	1.9	35.8
South Jamaica	35.6	60.0	53.0	4.9	84.6	4.3	61.5	5.3	27.6
Middle-income Areas									
Flushing	11.6	49.9	75.0	6.9	2.3	2.4	57.0	2.9	34.5
Richmond Hill	14.7	58.6	62.3	7.8	0.7	2.7	59.4	2.3	32.8
Averages									
New York City	29.0	61.0	42.5	9.5	14.7	5.0	58.1	3.2	32.1
Bronx	26.2	65.6	40.2	7.5	11.8	4.9	60.1	1.9	31.4
Brooklyn	26.1	62.6	43.6	9.3	14.5	5.1	58.7	2.4	33.4
Manhattan	34.4	64.2	19.7	4.0	25.1	6.9	55.1	5.7	29.9
Queens	14.4	56.5	66.2	6.7	8.5	3.0	58.6	2.8	32.4
Richmond	15.5	21.9	75.5	6.9	4.6	4.3	57.4	4.1	34.2

Source: 1960 Census of Population

Appendix Table 2

SUMMARY OF RAPID TRANSIT PASSENGERS,
BY STATIONS IN POVERTY AND NONPOVERTY AREAS
OF MANHATTAN AND THE BRONX

Manhattan, Annual

	YEARS ENDING JUNE 30			% Change 1955-60	% Change 1960-65
	1955	1960	1965		
NONPOVERTY AREAS					
Eighth Ave. Line N. of 59th St.	37,391,702	33,383,965	29,855,479	(10.7)	
Lenox Ave. Line	-	-	-	-	
Broadway Line	48,305,949	49,546,299	52,387,534	2.6	
Lexington Ave. Line	23,061,545	24,356,426	28,847,146	5.6	
TOTAL	108,759,196	107,286,690	110,090,159	(1.4)	2.6
POVERTY AREAS					
Eighth Ave. Line	31,692,154	27,674,816	23,491,586	(12.7)	
Lenox Ave. Line	14,384,984	14,735,632	15,637,049	2.4	
Broadway Line (125th St. only)	1,892,031	2,050,533	2,422,939	8.4	
Lexington Ave. Line	19,628,796	19,660,605	18,598,437	0.2	
TOTAL	67,597,965	64,121,586	60,150,011	(5.1)	(6.2)
TOTAL MANHATTAN (N. OF CBD)					
Eighth Ave. Line	69,083,856	61,058,781	53,347,065	(11.6)	
Lenox Ave. Line	14,384,984	14,735,632	15,637,049	2.4	
Broadway Line	50,197,980	51,596,832	54,810,473	2.8	
Lexington Ave. Line	42,690,341	44,017,031	46,445,583	3.1	
TOTAL	176,357,161	171,408,276	170,240,170	(2.8)	(0.7)

106

Bronx, Annual

YEARS ENDING JUNE 30

NONPOVERTY AREAS

	1955	1960	1965	% Change 1955-60	% Change 1960-65
Pelham Bay Line	14,544,850	15,575,310	16,192,537	7.1	
White Plains Road Line	12,662,419	12,847,472	13,610,533	1.5	
Dyre Ave. Line	1,488,816	2,586,407	3,348,191	73.7	
Third Ave. El Line	3,140,661	2,282,496	2,424,758	(27.3)	
Bronx Concourse Line	36,758,122	33,282,998	30,658,863	(9.5)	
Woodlawn Line	22,778,647	21,049,275	22,243,113	(7.6)	
Broadway Line	4,891,635	5,357,037	6,069,113	9.5	
TOTAL	96,265,150	92,980,995	94,547,108	(3.4)	1.7

POVERTY AREAS

	1955	1960	1965	% Change 1955-60	% Change 1960-65
Pelham Bay Line	15,167,333	16,758,259	15,618,780	10.5	
White Plains Road Line	30,968,804	30,835,229	31,115,336	(0.4)	
Third Ave. El Line	7,643,325	5,845,517	5,398,593	(23.5)	
Bronx Concourse Line	–	–	–	–	
Woodlawn Line	–	–	–	–	
Broadway Line	–				
TOTAL	53,779,462	53,439,005	52,132,709	(0.6)	(2.4)

TOTAL BRONX

	1955	1960	1965	% Change 1955-60	% Change 1960-65
Pelham Bay Line	29,712,183	32,333,569	31,811,317	8.8	
White Plains Road Line	43,631,223	43,682,701	44,725,869	0.1	
Dyre Ave. Line	1,488,816	2,586,407	3,348,191	73.7	
Third Ave. El Line	10,783,986	8,128,013	7,823,351	(24.6)	
Bronx Concourse Line	36,758,122	33,282,998	30,658,863	(9.5)	
Woodlawn Line	22,778,647	21,049,275	22,243,113	(7.6)	
Broadway Line	4,891,635	5,357,037	6,069,113	9.5	
TOTAL	150,044,612	146,420,000	146,679,817	(2.4)	0.2

(continued)

Appendix Table 2 (cont.)

Manhattan, Peak Period and Daily

	PEAK PERIOD [a]		24 HOURS		% CHANGE	
	1960 [b]	1965 [c]	1960	1965	Peak Period	24 Hours
NONPOVERTY AREAS						
Eighth Ave. Line N. of 59th St.	54,564	46,864	111,989	100,409	(14.1)	(10.3)
Lenox Ave. Line	-	-	-	-	-	-
Broadway Line	58,875	50,485	166,179	171,971	(14.2)	3.5
Lexington Ave. Line	17,182	20,078	87,234	102,765	16.8	17.8
TOTAL	130,621	117,427	365,402	375,145	(10.1)	2.7
POVERTY AREAS [a]						
Eighth Ave. Line	40,515	29,409	90,625	78,387	(27.4)	(13.5)
Lenox Ave. Line	21,819	19,858	47,701	47,361	(9.0)	(0.7)
Broadway Line (125th St. only)	2,284	2,599	6,920	7,510	13.8	8.5
Lexington Ave. Line	25,283	24,374	60,567	60,415	(3.6)	(0.3)
TOTAL	89,901	76,240	205,813	193,673	(15.2)	(5.9)
TOTAL MANHATTAN [b]						
Eighth Ave. Line	95,079	76,273	202.614	178,796	(19.8)	(11.8)
Lenox Ave. Line	21,819	19,858	47,701	47,361	(9.0)	(0.7)
Broadway Line	61,159	53,084	173,099	179,481	(13.2)	3.7
Lexington Ave. Line	42,465	44,452	147,801	163,180	4.7	10.4
TOTAL	220,522	193,667	571,215	568,818	(12.2)	(0.4)

Bronx, Peak Period and Daily

	PEAK PERIOD[a]		24 HOURS		% CHANGE	
	1960[b]	1965[c]	1960	1965	Peak Period	24 Hours
NONPOVERTY AREAS						
Pelham Bay Line	35,067	33,501	54,115	55,389	(4.5)	2.4
White Plains Road Line	24,911	24,938	44,476	46,658	0.1	4.9
Dyre Ave. Line	5,668	7,346	9,317	12,887	29.6	38.3
Third Ave. El Line	3,475	3,293	8,116	7,986	(5.2)	(1.6)
Bronx Concourse Line	64,977	54,749	114,732	103,746	(15.7)	(9.6)
Woodlawn Line	31,899	30,926	71,392	76,435	(3.1)	7.1
Broadway Line	9,326	10,435	18,892	19,968	11.9	5.7
TOTAL	175,323	165,188	321,040	323,069	(5.8)	0.6
POVERTY AREAS						
Pelham Bay Line	27,389	24,285	54,546	52,165	(11.3)	(4.4)
White Plains Road Line	49,257	45,560	94,252	96,190	(7.5)	2.1
Third Ave. El Line	10,540	9,084	19,606	18,388	(13.8)	(6.2)
Bronx Concourse Line	-	-	-	-	-	-
Woodlawn Line	-	-	-	-	-	-
Broadway Line	-	-	-	-	-	-
TOTAL	87,186	78,929	168,404	166,743	(9.5)	(1.0)
TOTAL BRONX						
Pelham Bay Line	62,456	57,786	108,661	107,554	(7.5)	(1.0)
White Plains Road Line	74,168	70,498	138,728	142,848	(4.9)	(3.0)
Dyre Ave. Line	5,668	7,346	9,317	12,887	29.6	38.3
Third Ave. El Line	14,015	12,377	27,722	26,374	(11.7)	(4.9)
Bronx Concourse Line	64,977	54,749	114,732	103,746	(15.7)	(9.6)
Woodlawn Line	31,899	30,926	71,392	76,435	(3.0)	7.0
Broadway Line	9,326	10,435	18,892	19,968	11.9	5.7
TOTAL	262,509	244,117	489,444	489,812	(7.0)	0.1

[a] 6 to 9 A.M.
[b] Wednesday, October 19, 1960.
[c] Wednesday, October 20, 1965.

Source: New York City Transit Authority, Transit Record.

Appendix Table 3

PER CENT DISTRIBUTION OF TOTAL DAILY NUMBER OF TRIPS ORIGINATING IN THE
BROWNSVILLE AREA OF CENTRAL BROOKLYN, BY MODE OF TRAVEL

Destination Areas	Per Cent Distribution Total Trips	Per Cent of Trips to Areas, by Mode of Travel		
		Public Transit[a]	Bus Only	Private Vehicle
Total All Trips	100.00	69.1	29.8	28.7
Total to Manhattan CBD	16.91	94.2	.6	5.8
Total Non-CBD	78.64	62.3	35.0	34.9
Upper East Side	.49	100.0	-	-
Upper West Side	.86	86.5	-	13.5
Spanish Harlem	.50	55.6	-	44.4
Harlem	.51	88.0	-	12.0
West Side-N. of Harlem	.40	71.6	-	28.4
Upper Manhattan	.06	100.0	-	-
TOTAL Manhattan N. of CBD	2.82	81.8	-	18.2
Botanical Gardens-Woodlawn	.06	100.0	-	-
High Bridge-Tremont University Heights	.39	72.1	-	27.9
Parkchester-Westchester Hts.	.05	100.0	-	-
Crotona Park-East Tremont	.11	47.6	-	52.4
South Bronx	.53	50.0	-	50.0
Classon Point-Castle Hill Pond	.06	100.0	-	-
Throgs Neck-Pelham Bay-City Island	.05	-	-	100.0
TOTAL Bronx	1.25	61.2	-	38.8
Greenpoint-Williamsburg	2.14	69.2	25.4	30.8
Bushwick	3.07	59.0	38.7	35.6
East New York	8.20	68.2	43.0	31.2
Brownsville	15.25	64.4	54.0	30.7
Brooklyn CBD-Crown Heights-Navy Yard	11.37	65.3	42.9	33.0

Destination Areas	Per Cent Distribution Total Trips	Per Cent of Trips to Areas, by Mode of Travel		
		Public Transit[a]	Bus Only	Private Vehicle
Red Hook-Park Slope-Prospect Park	5.97	72.7	39.2	26.4
Flatbush-Canarsie	9.04	56.1	47.8	36.3
Borough Park	1.90	80.0	22.3	20.0
Flatlands	2.40	51.0	26.8	49.0
Sheepshead Bay Area	1.58	46.1	16.1	50.3
Gravesend Bay Area	.82	52.6	21.6	47.4
Bay Ridge-New Utrecht	1.28	62.9	47.8	37.1
Brooklyn CBD	4.45	93.7	42.6	6.3
TOTAL Brooklyn	67.50	65.8	–	31.3
Long Island City-Astoria	1.25	91.2	–	8.8
Maspeth-Middle Village-Woodside-Elmhurst-Rego Park-Forest Hills	1.74	44.6	18.5	43.4
Jackson Heights-Corona	.55	61.5	–	38.5
College Pt.-Flushing-Whitestone	.59	54.5	–	45.5
Little Neck Bay	.06	–	–	100.0
Central Queens	.49	47.1	–	52.9
Woodhaven-Richmond Hill-Kew Gardens	.91	77.0	23.6	23.0
Eastern Queens	.20	25.1	–	74.9
Southeastern Queens	1.41	52.4	7.6	47.6
Aqueduct-Kennedy	1.04	72.5	12.1	27.5
Rockaway	.27	39.1	39.1	60.9
TOTAL Queens	8.51	60.6	10.3	37.0
Staten Island	–	–	–	–
Nassau County	2.12	10.9	–	89.1
Suffolk County	.35	–	–	100.0
Westchester County	.05	100.0	–	–
Rockland County	–	–	–	–
New Jersey	.47	44.6	–	55.4

[a] Subway, bus, and railroad.

APPENDIX C

MAPS AND STATISTICS OF
NEW YORK CITY'S
TRANSPORTATION SYSTEM

Appendix Figure 2

LOCATION OF NEW YORK CITY TRANSIT AUTHORITY AND
PATH RAPID TRANSIT STATIONS, SHOWING THEIR
PROXIMITY TO EMPLOYMENT AREAS

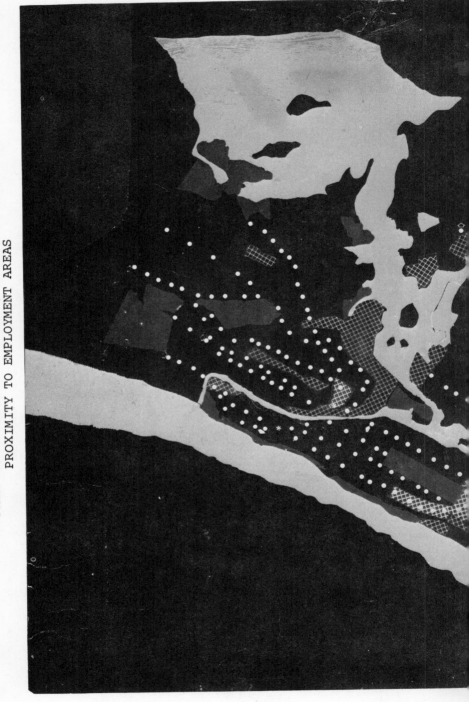

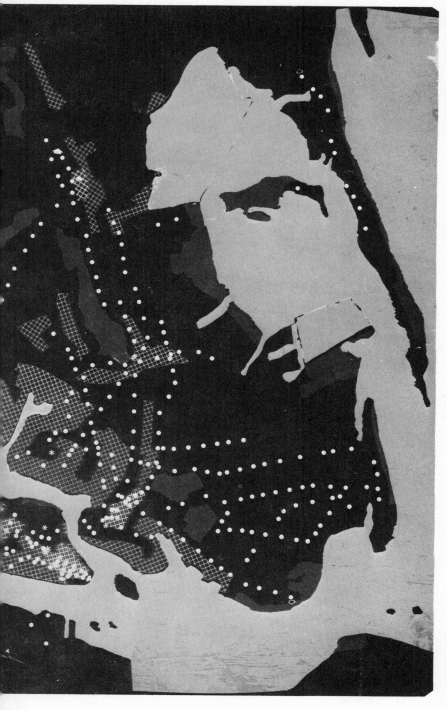

(continued)

Appendix Figure 2
(cont.)

Area A

116

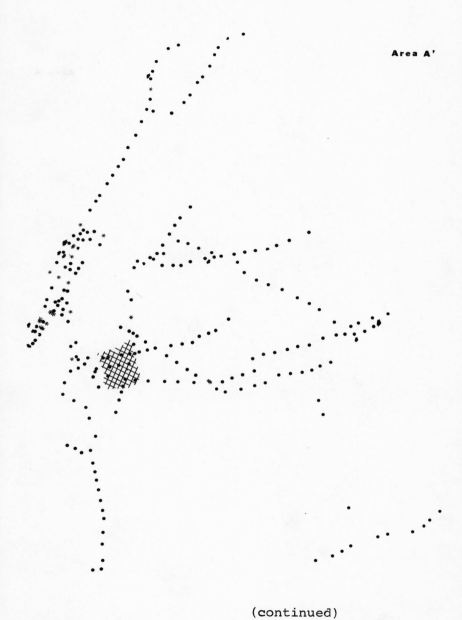

Area A'

(continued)

Appendix Figure 2
(cont.)

Area A"

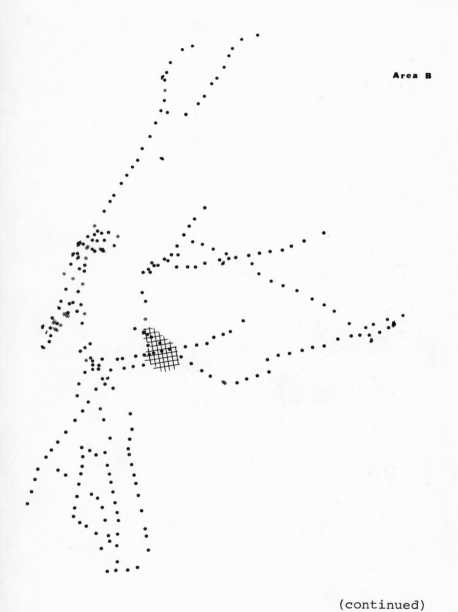

Area B

(continued)

Appendix Figure 2
(cont.)

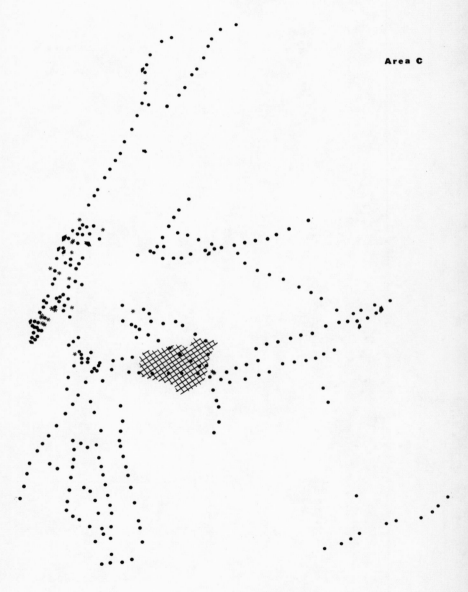

Area C

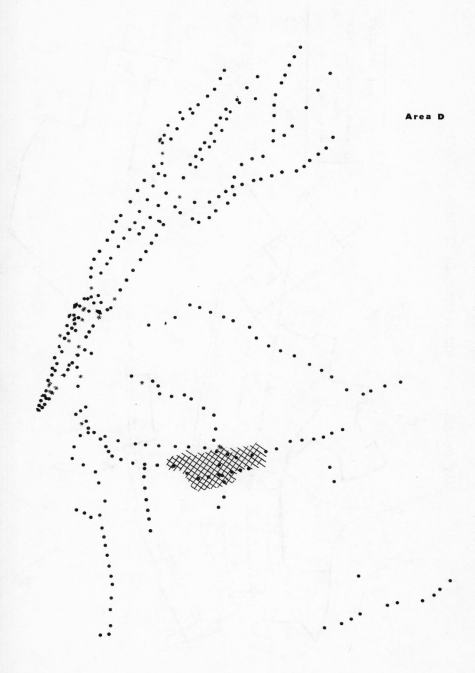

Area D

Appendix Figure 3

MAP OF SELECTED BUS ROUTES IN CENTRAL BROOKLYN

CENTRAL BROOKLYN
——— First Magnitude
Poverty Area Boundary
----- Bus Routes

Appendix Figure 4

PROPOSED EXPRESS BUS ROUTES FOR NEW YORK CITY POVERTY AREAS

Appendix Figure 5

COST FARE FRONTS FOR THE PUBLIC TRANSPORTATION
SYSTEM OF NEW YORK CITY

SELECTED BIBLIOGRAPHY

SELECTED BIBLIOGRAPHY

The problems of urban transportation and their relationship to the poor are discussed primarily in the following selected list of publications.

American Transit Association. Fact Book (yearly).

Budd, E. C. Inequality and Poverty. New York: W. W. Norton, 1967.

Chamber of Commerce of the United States. The Metropolitan Enigma. Washington, 1965.

Fitch, L. C. Urban Transportation and Public Policy. San Francisco: Chandler Publishing Company, 1964.

Ganz, A. Emerging Patterns of Urban Growth and Travel. Cambridge, Mass.: MIT Press, 1968.

Meyer, J. R., Kain, J. F., and Wohl, M. The Urban Transportation Problem. Cambridge, Mass.: Harvard Press, 1965.

National Bureau of Economic Research (NBER). Transportation Economics. New York: NBER, 1965.

Ornati, O. Poverty Amid Affluence. New York: Twentieth Century Fund, 1966.

Perloff, H.S. and Wingo, L. Issues in Urban Economics. Baltimore: Johns Hopkins Press, 1968.

Schneider, L.M. Marketing Urban Mass Transit. Cambridge, Mass.: Harvard University, 1965.

Thompson, W. R. A Preface to Urban Economics. Baltimore: Johns Hopkins Press, 1965.

Wingo, L. Transportation and Urban Land. Baltimore: Johns Hopkins Press, 1961.

ABOUT THE AUTHOR

Oscar A. Ornati is Professor of Management at the Graduate School of Business Administration of New York University. He is also Director of Project Labor Market, an ongoing study of the workings of New York City's labor market, previously funded by the City and now by The Ford Foundation. He has served as Chief of Economic Development and Manpower of the Office of Economic Opportunity and has been a consultant to various government agencies. He is currently vice president of Kirschner Associates, Inc., management consultants.

Prior to his current position, Professor Ornati was on the faculties of the New School for Social Research, Cornell University, Boston University, and Harvard College. During 1964-65, he was a member of the Mayor's Task Force Against Poverty in New York City; he presently is a member of the Board of Directors of the Upper Manhattan Small Business Development and Opportunities Corporation.

In the area of foreign labor, Dr. Ornati is a specialist on the labor situation in Italy, India, and Indonesia. He collaborated in developing the first eight-year economic development plan of the Republic of Indonesia. He has written extensively on poverty, urban problems, and labor relations. His previous publications include the books <u>Poverty Amid Affluence</u> and <u>Jobs and Workers in India</u> and numerous reports and journal articles.